W9-APK-290

SIMPLE WEALTH, INEVITABLE WEALTH

SIMPLE WEALTH, INEVITABLE WEALTH

NICK MURRAY

Copyright © 1999, 2004, 2008, 2010 Nicholas Murray
All rights reserved.

The Nick Murray Company, Inc.
www.nickmurray.com

No portion of this book may be used or reproduced in any manner whatsoever without written permission. The information in this publication does not constitute a recommendation for the purchase or sale of any securities. The author is not engaged in rendering investment advisory, legal or accounting services. If such assistance is required, seek the advice of a professional.

Printed in the United States of America.
Fourth edition: Thanksgiving 2010.

Library of Congress Catalog Card Number: 2004095298
ISBN: 0-9669763-4-7

This new edition is for
my brave, brilliant, beautiful daughter

JOAN EILEEN MURRAY

On the day that you were born, the angels got together
and decided to create a dream come true

TABLE OF CONTENTS

A Note on the Fourth Edition

MARK TWAIN'S CAT AND THE GREAT PANIC OF 2007 – 2009

Mark Twain memorably said that a cat, having once walked upon a hot stove, would never walk upon a hot stove again. ***Nor upon a cold stove.***

He was warning us, in his wonderfully sly way, against trying to learn too much from any one experience. Hold that thought, if you will, as I review some events which took place since the last edition of this book was published.

From its new closing high on October 9, 2007 to its panic-driven trough seventeen months later to the day, the broad equity market in the United States—as denominated in the Standard & Poor's 500-Stock Index—declined 57% on a closing basis. This rolling crash, which had no precedent in the memory of any but the oldest survivors of The Great Depression, was first set off by the vaporization of the market for an entirely new generation of exotic derivatives based on the single-family home market.

That was followed by the collapse of the housing market itself, then by the effective failure of the banking system, then by a total cessation of the global credit function, and finally by a deep and savage decline in the world economy, as the oxygen of credit was withdrawn from the planet. Governments ran up trillions of dollars of debt, trying to head off a financial nuclear winter—to no apparent avail.

Global investors fled the equity market as never before in modern memory. Some sold out of need: with the debt markets frozen, there was virtually no market for bonds at any rational price, such that selling stocks became the only practical way for institutions, companies and individuals to raise needed cash. But most sold out of pure panic—for, in the end, as it always does (and always will) in an epic decline, panic came to rule the markets.

By the first quarter of 2009, three financial indicators had reached levels rarely if ever seen. (1) As it continued its horrific free fall, the equity market finished wiping out all the returns it had produced in more than the previous ten years, *including that from dividends.* (2) The yield on U. S. Treasury bills of the shortest maturities was bidden down, by investors insatiably seeking safety, to zero. This was nothing more or less than a signal that they expected virtually all other risk assets *to produce a return of less than zero in the chaos that had enveloped the globe.* In plain English, zero looked good, so long as it took one's money out of harm's way.

Lastly (3), the sum of cash on deposit in money market funds and bank savings accounts—*not even counting certificates of deposit, just: money that could be withdrawn without penalty tomorrow*—came to exceed the total market capitalization of the Wilshire 5000 stock index, which purports to include substantially all the public companies in America. That is to say that Americans, using nothing but their cash on hand, could have reached out on any given day and bought all the publicly held common stock in the country. But of course, common stocks were, by then, the last thing in the world they would ever think of buying.

Whereupon a quite remarkable and almost totally unexpected thing happened. Seemingly against all reason and logic, **the world failed to end.**

Over the following thirteen months, almost as sharply as it had declined, global economic activity came roaring back. (Unemployment, always the last lagging indicator of recovery, remained agonizingly high, so of course unemployment was all journalism focused on.) The debt markets returned to relative normalcy. Corporate profits in this country soared, paced by startling gains in worker productivity. And the American equity market rose by something like 80% from its panic lows—a gain which, exactly like the decline which went before it, had no precedent since the 1930s.

As I write—and indeed this is precisely *why* I write—investors are still struggling to make sense of what happened, and to learn all that can be learned from these historic events.

What previously held theories and beliefs about investing

were disproven by the "lost decade," and how ought investors to alter their strategies? Did this historic bear market usher in a protracted period of low single-digit returns?

Is "buy and hold" dead? And if so, what strategy has replaced it? What have we learned, if anything, about how to allocate our assets between "risky" equities and "safe" bonds? How, in the future, might we get out of the markets early in such a terrible decline, and back in before we miss a significant recovery?

And finally: **if this terrifying volatility is the way equities really behave, are they even a rational place for the core savings of the "conservative" investor?**

These and a host of similar, seemingly very reasonable concerns all come down to the same question: ***what has changed, and how must we change in response?***

This book's answer—as it has consistently been since publication of the original edition in the bubble year 1999—is that, for the genuinely long-term, goal-focused investor, nothing has changed at all. The belief that "this time is different" was wrong then, and it was wrong at the bottom in 2009. The timeless approach to lifetime investing found in these pages in 1999—when the world was tripping out on "new era" greed and euphoria—is the same one you're about to read, after a historic orgy of global panic.

Then as now, the patient long-term seeker of wealth ought to focus not on things that appear to be changing, but on those things that have never changed. In exactly that sense, the key lesson of the Great Panic and commensurately great recovery of 2007–2009 is:

The world did not end *because it does not end.*

This priceless lesson is perhaps the spine of the book you're about to read. If you've learned it, there is some chance that you can save and invest your way to wealth—as you define the term—over the balance of your investing lifetime. (Even if you have not learned it, but are blessed to have a financial advisor who has, then you may still be all right.)

By the light of that epiphany, let's begin.

Somebody's sitting
in the shade today
because someone planted
a tree a long time ago.

—WARREN BUFFETT

PREFACE

In which the author states his biases and tells you how this book should be read

Over the course of the last four decades, I've been an advisor to individual investors, and now—for want of a better job description—am an advisor to other financial advisors. In this book, I will report to you absolutely everything of critical importance that I've learned about investing for the creation and maintenance of wealth.

That's the good news. Consider the possibility that it may also be the bad news.

It's potentially good news because if one labors diligently and lovingly at this profession for well over forty years—as I've tried my best to do—one learns an awful lot about how markets and investments really work. I need hardly add that, in investing as in life, one learns virtually all the great lessons the hard way. Heaven knows I did.

One also discovers the few big things that really matter in successful investing. One does this by experimenting with, and ultimately discarding, the multiplicity of stuff that turns out not to matter much, or to be just plain unknowable.

This painstaking (and occasionally painful) learning process prompted me, a decade or so ago, to say, "Let me write a little book for my fellow seekers of wealth, so that they may learn everything I know without having to make all my mistakes. And in that book, let me tell people only the ultimate essentials, so that they don't have to waste a lot of time and energy learning to filter out the noise." Simplicity, said the immortal Leonardo, is the ultimate sophistication. And this book is my attempt to bring you directly to that happy state, without detours, stopovers, or too much heavy lifting.

That pretty much concludes the good news. The other news—and it may not be bad, so much as it is cautionary—is this. Against just about every point this book makes, there's a significant counter-argument. These counter-arguments are often persuasively made, and by quite credible people. Here are just three pertinent examples.

- Many reputable portfolio managers, authors and financial planners believe that you should allocate your invested assets among stocks, bonds and cash, particularly as you get older. They argue that this strategy strikes an appropriate balance between your need for good returns and your need for stability, and for protection of capital. ***I couldn't disagree more.*** I believe that if wealth is truly your goal, stocks aren't part of the answer, they're the only answer because—net of inflation and taxes—they're the only financial asset that has any return. Not just a better return, mind you: ***any*** return.

- You will hear powerful arguments for selecting and owning individual stocks, versus investing in managed and/or indexed portfolios of stocks. Peter Lynch made this case, as cogently and charmingly as I've ever seen it made, in his first book, *Beating the Street*. ***I couldn't disagree more.*** I believe that most investors (not all, just most) will get much better returns from mutual funds and other pooled and managed portfolios—that is, from owning portfolios of stocks rather than trying to select individual stocks on their own.

- Just about everywhere you look these days—in books, magazines, cable and the blogosphere—you'll see strong suggestions that you manage your investment portfolio on your own, without the involvement (or the cost) of a financial advisor. ***I couldn't disagree more.*** All my years and all my experience tell me that most investors will achieve far superior lifetime results—with far less pain and suffering—working with a caring, competent and above all trusted financial advisor.

These are my, and therefore this book's, most deeply held core beliefs. The point is that you're entitled to treat them as my biases, and therefore you needn't take them at face value. I've labored to present both sides of each issue as fairly as I can. But—especially as respects the critical need for an advisor—you already know, given my background, where I'm going to come out. In fact, you don't know the half of it.

I know that the principles and practices in this book are most families' best chance to achieve and preserve wealth. But in order for this book to work for you, you're going to have to believe it almost as deeply as I do. This isn't a cafeteria, where you pick what looks tasty, and pass the other dishes by. If you miss one vital link in the chain of logic, the chain may—and, at a critical market turning point, almost certainly will—break. Please don't flirt with this stuff. Come all the way in, or stay all the way out.

Some other suggestions for reading the book:

- Understand that this book uses mutual funds as a proxy for the whole panoply of equity-based portfolios: separately managed accounts, the sub-accounts of variable life insurance and variable annuity contracts, closed-end and exchange-traded funds, and so forth. Every investor must, with an advisor's counsel, weigh the benefits and the costs of these different approaches. *I'm writing about equity investing, not about any particular box in which equities may be packaged.* In this book, therefore, equity mutual funds simply stand in for all the different boxes.

- Relax. Try to read this book straight through once just for enjoyment. Investing is supposed to make you feel good, and so is this little book. So take it easy, and have some fun with it.

- This book isn't primarily about answers, or at least not about the answers you may be looking for ("Which six funds should I buy now?"). It's about making sure you get the really important questions framed right. Smart people in general, and good investors in particular, realize that you can never find the right answers until you're sure you're asking the right questions. (Examples: What are stocks? What is risk? What does wealth mean to me? *Who am I?*)

- This book doesn't say that your mutual funds are going to "outperform" most other people's mutual funds. *It says that you are going to achieve much better results than do most other people.* Seeing that these are two different things—that the key to "outperforming" most other people is simply **behaving more appropriately than they do**—is the beginning of wisdom. Scratch golfers don't necessarily hit the largest number of great shots; they hit the fewest really terrible shots. To an extent that may astonish you, exceptional results in equity investing proceed from avoiding a few really awful—but awfully common—mistakes.

- Any book for a general audience about an apparently technical subject like investing is going to be too complicated for some readers and too basic for others. If you find yourself falling into the latter category ("too basic"), I'd like politely to suggest the possibility that what you may be looking for either doesn't matter or doesn't exist.

> To the former group ("too complicated") let me plead that I have avoided jargon and math as much as I could. And every time I've used a word or phrase you might not recognize, I've defined it in a Glossary at the back of the book. If, even at that, this book still seems too complex, run—do not walk—to a financial advisor.

Now, before you read on, I'd like you to close the book for a few moments, and look at the image on the front cover. I'll wait here for you.

Welcome back. Yes, that's right: it's a tree. It's not the imposing façade of the New York Stock Exchange, or a computer screen full of numbers, or a frenzied trading floor, or anything like that. It's a tree. You plant it in the earth, and a wonderful force of nature causes it to take root, and to grow. You don't have to do much with it: the air and the water and the nutrients it needs are all around the tree, and it knows how to use them.

You don't dig it up every ninety days to check on its progress. (Nothing much will have changed in that brief time, and you might harm the tree.) You don't uproot the tree and store it in your garage over the winter, to protect it from what you regard as "bad weather." (Though its leaves fall and it stops growing for a season, the tree itself does not die. And even leafless, the tree is still producing oxygen, without which you and I could not live.)

Give the tree enough room, enough light, and enough time. Then leave it pretty much alone. It will give you back air and shade and beauty as it grows—and will go on doing so for your children, after you're gone.

That's what investing is like—if you let it be. Wealth is no less organic than that tree; the growth of wealth in equity mutual funds is no less a force of nature. So here's my last tip on how to read this book.

Take it outside. Go sit under a tree. Read it slowly. Read it well. Know that time and nature are on your side. And know that it is a friend who is writing to you.

FOREWORD

What this book will do for you, and what it won't

Wealth is freedom.

It isn't a thing, nor is it any accumulation of things. Above all, it isn't a certain number of dollars of net worth. There are, after all, families who would feel themselves inexpressibly wealthy to have accumulated an invested net worth of $500,000, and others for whom five million wouldn't begin to be enough.

Wealth is freedom. At the very least, wealth frees you from financial worry about what will happen to you, and perhaps to your children. No matter how much money you have, if you're still worried, you aren't wealthy. Freedom from financial fear is thus wealth's great negative accomplishment.

Beyond that, wealth is the positive freedom to live the kind of life that is meaningful to you, even—and especially—when you no longer work to earn an income. When your investments, as distinctly opposed to the sweat of your brow, will provide you sufficient income to live a full and joyful life, then you are truly wealthy—because you are truly free.

Moreover, if your investments continue to grow, even as you draw all the retirement income you need to support an uncompromised life, you'll be able to bequeath some measure of your financial freedom to the people you love, and must leave behind in the world. Surely that ability is the ultimate wealth, regardless of how many or how few dollars are involved. There are even those among us who think of it as a kind of immortality.

This book says two fundamental things. First, the process of achieving wealth, as you've just seen wealth defined, is actually quite simple—probably much simpler than you think.

Note that I did not say it was easy, because it certainly isn't. Though the principles and methods in this book are simple, they are at times almost unbearably difficult to stick to. Faith in these principles, as well as the patience and discipline to continue practicing them *no matter what happens*, are qualities which most people simply cannot sustain. That's why most investors fail to become wealthy.

But—and here is the book's second fundamental premise—if you *can* keep faith with these few simple principles, wealth is inevitable in the long run.

Take another deep breath. Try to relax just a little bit more. Open yourself up—perhaps for the first time in your life—to the possibility that both these extraordinary statements are true. (1) It is *simple* to accumulate wealth through patient, disciplined investment in equity mutual funds—those which invest primarily if not exclusively in common stocks. (2) If history is any guide—and it's the only guide we have—provided that you will give your equity investment plan both enough time and enough money, wealth is ultimately *inevitable*.

Note, please, that these statements are true **regardless of how little knowledge of economics or the markets you bring to the effort.** The system in this book—if we can even call it that—requires no special expertise, and demands very little of your time and energy. Wealth, you will discover, is much less a function of what you know than of what you do.

Much more than this, no one can truthfully say. There is no magic formula. There is no miracle cure, no short cut to wealth in equities. If you have $200,000 in capital, are three years from retirement, and have suddenly figured out that you'll need a total of $750,000 to retire on comfortably, neither this book nor anything else can reliably make that happen.

This is not to suggest that it is impossible to turn $200,000 into $750,000 in equity mutual funds in three years. Perhaps you will bet it all on some sector of the market that becomes blazing hot over the next block of time. It's possible. In very much the same sense, it is possible that you will win the lottery, or that a relative you didn't even know you had will die, and leave you the required $550,000.

But these strokes of good fortune aren't even remotely *probable*, much less inevitable, and therefore fall outside the scope of this book.

Similarly, if you're thirty years old, and plan to invest $250 a month until you're sixty, at which time your goal is to have a total accumulation of $5 million, neither I nor anyone else can hold you out any reasonable hope of getting there.

What I *can* say is that if you invest your $250 a month for thirty years, earn a 10% average return (which is about what the Standard & Poor's 500-Stock Index has done over the last 84 years), immediately reinvest all your dividends and capital gains in more fund shares, and pay taxes out of your own pocket rather than out of your investments, you'll have $519,823 at age 60. This isn't $5 million, but it ain't chopped liver, either.

Incidentally, if you invested $2,405 a month for thirty years—same 10% return, same other assumptions—you'd have your $5 million. This gives you a small insight into the staggering power of long-term compounding, which is one of equities' greatest benefits. Einstein wasn't kidding—well, he wasn't *just* kidding—when he said that mankind's greatest invention was compound interest.

And finally, in the interest of complete disclosure, let it be noted that if you invest your $250 a month for the next thirty years, and get an average return not of 10% but 19%, you will indeed reach your $5 million. Again: possible—if only in the sense that nothing is impossible—but not even remotely probable. Somewhere you may find a book which will tell you that you can reliably earn that kind of return; this is certainly not that book.

I know how you can grow wealth—an income you don't outlive, a significant legacy to your children and grandchildren—both simply and, in the long run, inevitably. Moreover, I know how your heirs can keep that wealth growing through succeeding generations. This book will communicate that knowledge to you in terms you cannot fail to understand. *But it will not do anything else.*

Investing is one aspect—but only one aspect—of a comprehensive financial and estate plan. *A portfolio is not, in and of itself, a plan.* And a portfolio that isn't in service to a plan is just a form of speculation; it can have no other goal than to beat most other people's portfolios.

But "outperformance" isn't a financial goal. An income you don't outlive—to cite one critical example—is a financial goal. If your portfolio "outperforms" mine, such that I run out of money when I'm 75, and you don't run out of money until you're 82, it isn't going to matter much when we're both 85, sitting on a park bench without two nickels to rub together between us.

You need a financial plan, which means you need a financial planner, and we will examine that vital issue in the next chapter. This book is essentially (and quite deliberately) silent on all those aspects of planning—budgeting, mortgages, managing your installment and revolving debt, life and disability insurance, wills, trusts, and a half dozen other issues—which fall outside the area of investing.

I also take no position in the matter of how your equity investments should be held—in a traditional IRA, a Roth IRA, a 401(k) plan, in a personal account, in a trust, or none of the above. This, again, is a fairly complex planning issue, and again, it has to be addressed with a trusted advisor who will take the time thoroughly to understand you and your family. No book can do that—not mine, not anyone else's.

Finally, as far as selecting specific equity mutual funds is concerned, this book forgoes any detailed discussion, for a very simple—and perhaps startling—reason: **in the great scheme of things, fund selection just isn't that important.**

No one is ever going to achieve wealth, or fail to achieve it, because of which particular equity funds he owned. Selecting stock funds which prove to be superior can surely cause you to become wealthi***er***, but this can never be the make-or-break issue.

The critical issue is: did you invest relentlessly in *any* stock funds as opposed to any bond funds, individual bonds, or CDs. The overarching truth about wealth is that it comes to, and abides with, the owners of great companies, not the lenders to great companies. I'm not suggesting that an owner cannot lose; *I'm declaring as an article of faith that a loaner can't win.*

Beyond that, though, the importance of specific fund selection is relatively small, when compared to the issue of how the investor herself behaves. If you are constantly diving into funds with spectacular performance over the previous few years, then switching funds as yours go cold and new hot performers grab the headlines, and finally selling out in revulsion and fear when your funds decline in value by a third and more in a perfectly normal "bear market"—you not only won't become wealthy, you'll lose much of the capital you've saved. Think of it, dear reader: one can buy nothing but top-rated funds, and yet lose significant amounts of money, *if one's own behavior is sufficiently inappropriate.* Indeed, it's done all the time.

The converse is, gloriously, also true. If you steadily accumulate even mundane stock funds month after month and year after year, if you patiently remain true to your tortoise disciplines in a wildly rising market even as hares go whizzing past you left and right, and above all if you regard declining markets as opportunities to buy more of your funds at sale prices rather than as the onset of Armageddon—you'll not only achieve wealth, you'll probably "outperform" 90% of your fellow investors without even trying.

Thus, a huge percentage of your total lifetime return will be attributable to the simple decision to be an owner and not a loaner—that is, to be a stock investor rather than a bond investor. And most of the rest of your real-life return depends not on how your stock funds perform versus their peers, but on how you yourself behave. ***Wealth isn't primarily determined by investment performance, but by investor behavior.***

This imposes a certain responsibility on you—and on your advisor, who will be your behavioral coach—but you should also find it intensely liberating. Investors who feel that their financial fate is a hostage to the vagaries of global economics, or impersonal market forces, or the personalities of their fund mangers whom they don't really know, often see themselves as pawns, and even victims. And victims don't win. But investors who correctly realize that their own behavior is the decisive variable in their long-term results feel—because in fact they are—very much in control of their own destinies. As you will be, by the time you finish reading this book.

And that, when all is said and done, is why the book is almost totally devoted to shaping and pointing your core beliefs and behaviors, rather than to a refinement like fund selection—which is much better done by you and a financial advisor who knows and cares about you.

Incidentally, if the truth that fund selection has relatively little to do with the achievement of wealth strikes you as novel—and even heretical—it's because the world around you conspires to obscure this message. After all, the great bulk of the financial input you get all day is essentially journalistic. And journalism, by its nature, stays in business by selling you the news—which is timely—as opposed to the truth, which is timeless.

The ninth time in a row that any investing magazine headlined the timeless truths—"Own, don't loan; stay diversified; don't chase hot fads; don't panic out; faith, patience and discipline; slow and steady wins the race; end of story!"—it would go out of business, because people would have gotten the message and wouldn't need to read it anymore. To survive, a magazine has to keep blaring, "Six Hot Funds To Buy Now!" And of course, they're always six different funds. This helps the magazine, but hurts the investor. We will have much more to say about the evils of financial journalism as this book unfolds. For the moment, try to remember the last time somebody told you he got wealthy by reading *Money* magazine or watching CNBC.

This brings us to the final introductory point regarding what this book will do for you and what it won't. It is a point that is absolutely essential not just to the logic of the book, but to the probability that the book will actually work for you in the long run. Simply stated, most households and families will be much more successful at achieving and then preserving wealth with the help of a caring and competent financial advisor than by trying to do it themselves.

Fund selection is, or ought to be, the smallest part of what a gifted advisor does for you. We've already seen that, as important as a portfolio is, it only makes sense as the servant of a plan—ideally, a comprehensive, written financial and estate plan, but at the very least a lifetime investment plan.

Taking the time to understand you and your family emotionally as well as financially, building that overall plan and helping you fund it with the right kinds of investments, and guiding you past all the fads and fears of an investing lifetime—serving, in effect, as your own in-house "appropriate behavior" coach—that's what the great advisors do. They are much more focused on your life than on the markets. And their value to you is many times their cost, which is—or certainly ought to be—your main concern.

Can you achieve wealth, as this book defines it, without such an advisor/coach? It's possible. Should you try? Almost certainly not. The entire quality of your later life, and of your heirs' lives, is riding on this—while estate and tax laws, the global economy and markets, and the bewildering array of investment choices grow daily more complex.

Don't try to go it alone. The stakes are too high; the road is too long and often very dark. (Remember: it's simple, but it sure isn't easy). The cost of help is too negligible compared to the benefits, especially at critical moments. And the number of absolutely wonderful people in the financial advisor community—ethical, knowledgeable, caring people—is too great.

So before we talk about anything else, let me tell you how to identify, and work successfully with, the advisor who's right for you.

Risk is not knowing what you're doing.

—WARREN BUFFETT

Chapter One

WHAT YOUR FINANCIAL ADVISOR CAN DO FOR YOU, AND WHAT HE CAN'T

I you own this book, it is in all probability because a financial advisor recommended it to you—if she didn't actually give it to you outright.

Such is the way in which, over the last ten years, about 150,000 copies of this book found their way into the hands of people all over the English-speaking world. (Ask anyone in the publishing industry how a self-published book, sold without advertising or marketing of any kind, not in bookstores but only out of the author's office, can possibly sell 150,000 copies. They will cheerfully assure you that it can't.)

If there's one key to the acceptance this little book has found, it's probably in the fact that it may be the only book of any consequence in English which demonstrates that—and why—wealth in equities as we have defined it is practically impossible without the steady guidance of a gifted financial advisor.

The operative word in the foregoing sentence is, of course, *practically.*

You can, theoretically, make a lifetime financial and investment plan yourself, fund it with an appropriately diversified portfolio of the right kinds of equity funds, and blissfully accumulate your way to wealth, ignoring all the manias and panics which will surely afflict the markets between now and the time you retire. You can then—still all on your own—

decide how those assets are to be deployed in retirement, such that you can withdraw a lifestyle-sustaining income that keeps up with the ever-increasing cost of living, and still leaves a meaningful legacy to your heirs. None of this is, strictly speaking, impossible. The question: is it **probable?**

My experience indicates that it's not. I know two truths, and believe that they're decisive. First, there is a qualified, caring, committed financial advisor for you. Second, the value of that advisor to you and your family—in incremental return, in mistakes not made, in time and worry you needn't expend trying to do it yourself—will greatly exceed the cost of the advice.

Left to your own devices, I believe you'd almost certainly draw the same conclusion. "It's OK if I mow my own lawn, paint my own house and change my own spark plugs," you would reason. "I've got the time, I can save a few bucks, I need the exercise, and besides, I kind of enjoy puttering around with that stuff.

"On the other hand, I probably don't want to do surgery on my own aorta, nor draw up my own estate plan. Too tricky; too much riding on the outcome. The cost is money well spent, because of the years added to my life by my expertly patched aorta, or the estate taxes saved by my professionally drawn estate plan. Oh, yeah, and investing: who has the time or the temperament or the expertise to do their own investing?"

You *would* reason this way—if you weren't constantly bombarded with ads and articles to the effect that you're better off doing your own research, that it's cheaper, and that you don't have to risk the terrible experiences you'll have with the cartoon flim-flam stockbrokers in those trade-for-yourself commercials. (It is always very telling, to me, that the trade-for-yourself ads don't feel that they can convince you with a recitation of their capabilities and pricing. They have to sell against grotesque, straw-man caricatures of full-service advisors. Ah, but there I go again, demonstrating my biases.)

The premises of all do-it-yourself appeals are (1) that most investors are smart enough, rational enough and disciplined enough always to select and maintain portfolios that are best suited to their long-term goals, and (2) that most advisors are venal and/or stupid—or, at the very least, cost much more than they're worth. The former premise is a fundamental misreading of basic human nature; the latter is just a self-serving, mean-spirited lie.

These days, a professional investment advisor probably costs somewhere in the neighborhood of one percent per year, expressed as a percentage of the assets you have under her management. That one percent is over and above the management fees and expenses of the mutual funds (or whatever equity portfolios) you own, *which you would pay anyway, even if you owned those funds/portfolios without an advisor.*

We're just solving, here, for a general sense of what professional investment advice costs.

You might find that cost to be a few tenths of a percent more on smaller portfolios (say, under $100,000), or a few tenths of a percent less on larger ones (say, north of $5 million). But let's simply agree that, in some form or fashion, an advisor today annually costs about one percent of your invested assets, which you would not have to pay if you did it yourself.

The only worthwhile question, then, is: **will an advisor directly cause your long-term, real-life return to exceed by more than one percent per year the return you would achieve on your own?**

If you think an advisor *would* add more than one percent (or whatever he costs) to your probable do-it-yourself experience—that, simply stated, his advice will be worth more to you than it costs—it would be irrational not to employ one. And of course, if you think he could not possibly cover his cost by an appreciable margin, then there'd be no sense in hiring him.

There are, it seems to me, three areas in which a professional advisor might add significant value to your probable do-it-yourself outcome. (1) He might increase your return by more than one percent a year by creating a portfolio which is better suited to your long-term goals than the one you'd select, left to your own resources. (2) He might save you the equivalent of one percent a year in the time, energy and worry that go into managing your own investments. And finally (3) he might actually save you some multiple of one percent a year, by coaching you out of making the great behavioral mistakes—throwing too much money at an investment fad near its top, or panicking completely out of equities near a bottom, to cite just two—which cause most investors not merely to underperform the markets, *but to underperform their own investments.*

Again, if you conclude that the combined contribution of these three services would probably be worth more than one percent to you, you've made the case for having an advisor. **If you even suspect that *each* of these three contributions might be worth anything like one percent, then engaging an advisor becomes heaven's own original no-brainer.** And if all your instincts cry out that no advisor, even in the act of delivering these three blessings, would cause your results to improve by more than one percent a year—well, you probably ought to just skip ahead to the next chapter. And good luck to you.

These are the big things a personal advisor can do. In the very next breath, let's make sure you know beyond a shadow of a doubt the three important things he cannot do, ***because nobody can.***

(1) An advisor cannot, with any consistency or precision, forecast the economy. No one can. (2) He cannot, with any consistency or precision, forecast the markets, much less time them. No one can. (3) He cannot, based on their past relative performance, forecast the future relative performance of similar mutual funds or other equity portfolios. ***No one can.***

Abandon, here and now, the toxic illusion that the proper function of an investment advisor is any form of prediction, or any method of selection for consistently superior "performance." **The great advisors deal not in prediction and "performance," but in planning, perspective and behavioral coaching.** They will cheerfully tell you that that's why they were sent into the world. They will assure you—as I already have, and will again—that the dominant determinant of long-term, real-life investment outcomes is not the performance of investments *but the behavior of investors.* And that therefore they—the great advisors—are planners rather than prognosticators, who don't manage portfolios *so much as they manage people.*

Do all advisors approach their craft, and relate to their clients, through these beliefs and practices? Even today, I think, most still do not. And are there not venal and/or stupid advisors? Surely there are, just as there are venal and stupid attorneys, accountants and physicians. The important thing is that now you know how the stupid and/or venal advisor will come at you.

He will claim the ability to forecast the economy, and therefore the ability to jump in and out of the markets opportunely. He will promise that, by timing the markets and/or by identifying superior funds, he is going consistently to "outperform" on your behalf. He will assert his ability to deliver "higher returns with less risk," whatever that's alleged to mean at any given moment. The only difference—and it's no real difference at all, as far as you're concerned—is that the stupid advisor will genuinely still believe he can do these things. The venal advisor will long since have discovered that he can't, but will continue nonetheless to claim that he can, because that's what he thinks you want to hear.

The quality advisor—the one you want, and the one whom, if he gave you this book, I suspect you've already got—begins by learning everything he can about your hopes, dreams, goals and financial capabilities. Then he makes a plan with and for you. I hope and expect that this will be a comprehensive financial and estate plan (for which, I should mention, there may very well be a separate charge), but at the very least it will be a lifetime investment plan.

Then and only then he will build you a portfolio, *based not on an economic or market outlook—which he won't have—but on the dictates of the plan.* Finally, he will coach you—with a lot of empathy but also with a lot of tough love—past the emotional pitfalls of an investing lifetime: the fads, fears and misconceptions which relentlessly attack us all, year after year for the rest of our lives, not because we are unintelligent but because we are human.

If your goal is wealth as we've defined it—an income you don't outlive in a dignified and independent retirement, followed by meaningful legacies to those you love and must leave behind in the world—your advisor will almost certainly tell you that the preponderance of your lifetime portfolio will need to be in equities, not bonds. In the next three chapters—which form the core of this book and this philosophy—we'll discover what your advisor is going to say about this...and why he's right.

But just before we embark on that journey, let me make absolutely sure that you've already intuited what the only sustainable basis for a successful advisor/client relationship can possibly be. That basis is implicit mutual respect and trust. That's the only way it's ever going to work.

I certainly don't wish to minimize the importance of competence on the advisor's part; far from it. I simply want to stress that competence can never be the decisive issue.

First of all, competence, in an uncertain world, can take you only so far. As we've already begun to see, no matter how "smart" your advisor is, she still can't tell you what the economy or the markets are going to do next, how to get out at the top and back in at the bottom, and which large-company growth fund is going to outperform all its peers over the next five years...because no one can. Moreover, the qualities of intelligence and integrity are not necessarily related to each other in any meaningful way, as was amply demonstrated by the financial geniuses at Enron, and especially by the peerless Mr. Bernard Madoff.

So I'm all for competence, as far as it goes. But it will never sustain a successful relationship between you and your advisor. When you most want a left-brain, analytical, intellectual answer ("How will the current 'crisis' end, and when will the market stop going down?"), he will have only right-brain, perspective-based answers. ("I can't tell you how, when or even why this decline will stop. I can only tell you ***that*** it will stop. The world is not ending, *because it does not end. **Stand by our plan.***") That will be the crucial moment in the relationship; it may very well be the critical turning point in your investing career. And what happens in that moment will be a pure function of the extent to which you believe and trust your advisor.

What your advisor owes you is his full attention when he's dealing with you, a keen interest in helping you reach your financial goals, a proper respect for your fears and concerns (though his greatest value to you will be in helping you not give in to those fears), and the patience to explain his solutions to you in language you can understand, without patronizing you. What you owe your advisor is faith in his judgment—particularly when his faith in the future seems so at odds with current events.

Of such mutual respect and trust is enduring wealth built.

Just Remember

- The value to you of a good advisor greatly exceeds what he costs. That's all that matters.

- Assume that good advice costs about one percent a year, expressed as a percentage of your portfolio. If a high-quality advisor can *either* help you increase your return by more than that, *or* save you more than that in time, effort and worry, *or* save you more than that by preventing you from making the classic mistakes...she's worth it. If the advisor can do *all* those things—*and she very well might*—then hiring a coach is a no-brainer.

- The great advisors build portfolios based on their clients' goals, not on a view of the economy or the markets. They deal in planning and long-term perspective, not in prognostication.

- Advisors can neither forecast the economy, nor time the markets, nor say for sure which equity mutual fund will outperform its peers. ***No one can.*** So regardless of the way the markets are zigging or zagging at any given moment, expect your advisor to take the position that if your goals haven't changed (and they haven't), and if your portfolio was built to fund those most cherished long-term goals (and it was), then there is probably no compelling reason to change the portfolio.

- You may not always understand this advice, and you may even find your emotions straining against it. At such times, you'll realize why ***mutual trust and respect are the only basis for a sustainable, successful advisor/client relationship.*** At the end of the day, your coach's advice has to be trusted, even—and especially—when you don't fully agree with it.

- Try not to worry. Your advisor is doing that for you. Indeed, she's doing it for all her clients—more so, perhaps, than you can imagine. So if, at the beginning of your journey together, you both agreed that she would drive, *resist the impulse to grab the steering wheel.*

There is nothing new
in the world except
the history you
do not know.

—HARRY S. TRUMAN

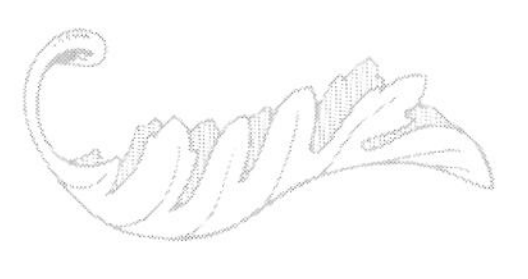

Chapter Two

AN OWNER, NOT A LOANER

In trying to understand any problem, you're always well advised to break it down into its component parts. By mastering smaller, bite-sized aspects of the problem, you have a better chance to comprehend the whole.

So let it be with equity mutual funds, which are actually a combination of two completely separate issues: equities (common stocks) and mutual funds.

Try to think of equities as the best birthday present you ever got in your whole life. Now try to think of mutual funds as the box your present came in. I don't care how unique or attractive that box and its wrapping were; the thing that warmed and cheered and thrilled you—and the one thing into which the giver put the most love and care—was the present, not the box.

This chapter begins an extended discussion of your birthday present: equities. All in good time, we'll sort through the issues concerning the box and the wrapping. Just see, for the moment, that the box/wrapping/mutual fund concerns are separate from, and far less important than, the essential questions of what equities are, how they work, and why they are indispensable to the seeker of real wealth.

Equity—common stock—is nothing more or less than a share in the ownership of a business. (Thus it is not, among many other things, a casino chip or a lottery ticket. There's a world of difference between an investment and a bet.) Your common sense and your life experience will tell you that it is the owners of good businesses who achieve real wealth in this country.

Think about it. Nearly everyone you've ever known about who achieved lasting financial independence owned a business, or was a manager and/or a stockholder in a business. In a capitalist economy, that's the way it's supposed to work. And in America—the greatest capitalist economy that ever was or ever will be—that's exactly how it does work.

To start or expand her business, the owner might very well have taken a loan. The lender got a certain amount of security for his loan in the form of some kind of collateral. He also got a stated rate of return in the form of an interest rate on the loan. But no matter how profitable the business may become, the lender doesn't participate in those profits. On the other hand, if the business is unprofitable for a long enough period of time, and the owner can't repay the loan, the lender will foreclose on the collateral.

The lender to a business takes only the risk that the collateral won't be enough to repay the loan. And, if he's done his job right, this shouldn't be much of a risk at all. Having taken not much risk, the lender appropriately receives...not much return. And no chance at all to hit a home run if the business really takes off.

The owner of the business takes a good deal more risk than the lender. If she can't repay the loan, she'll see the major assets of her business—if not the business itself—taken away. Of course, if she succeeds she gets to keep all the profits, and all of the increased value in her prospering business, above and beyond the face amount of the loan and the interest she has to pay the lender.

Makes perfect sense, doesn't it? Indeed, even if you've never owned a share of stock or a mutual fund in your life—much less a business—there's still a good chance that you have personal experience of how wealth comes to the owner and not the loaner. It's called buying a home, and taking a mortgage to do so.

In the 1970s, my family and I bought our first home. We paid $80,000 for it, which seemed to us like all the money in the world at the time. Our down payment was $20,000 and we borrowed $60,000 from a bank in the form of a thirty-year mortgage.

Twenty years later, almost to the day, we sold that home for $627,500. OK, we'd done some significant improvements over the years, so let's say that, apples to apples, our $80,000 became $500,000 in a little over twenty years.

What did the lender get? All his principal back (we'd long

since paid off the mortgage) and a fixed rate of interest. What did we get? All—not some of, not most of, *all*—the appreciation in the home. The bank made a very good loan, but we made a truly great buy.

(If this all seems logical to you, then you've already got a pretty good handle on the concept of owner vs. loaner. You might just want to pause a moment here, take another deep breath, and pat yourself on the back. Even if you opened this book saying, "Hell, I don't know the difference between a stock and a bond," what we've just demonstrated is: yes, you do. See, I *told* you this was going to be simple, but you didn't want to believe me…)

OK, we know in concept that the lender to a business—the bondholder—doesn't take much risk and doesn't get much return. We know, too, that the owner of the business—the stockholder—takes more risk than the lender and gets more (and maybe a whole lot more) return. The next step is to move beyond the concept and see if we can find out just how much more return the stockholder gets, and just how much more risk she takes.

And here we run smack into the next major idea—one that we all have to know and accept—about investing (and, for that matter, about life). ***It is the essential unknowability of the future.***

Deciding whether to invest in stocks or bonds, and in what mix, would be a lot easier if we could be sure what those two asset classes were going to return, relative to each other, over the balance of our investing lifetime. As with every other aspect of the future (including whether the sun's coming up tomorrow, and whether we'll be here to see it if it does), this knowledge is unavailable to us. "Certainty" is not a condition that exists in nature. Reasonable probability, based on an examination of historical bond/stock relationships, is all we have, and it will therefore have to do. The further we look back, Winston Churchill said, the further we may see ahead.

Let's look first at the absolute returns of certain asset classes for the period January 1, 1926 through December 31, 2009. This is the period for which we have the most reliable information—before that the data get kind of fuzzy—and you'll find most professional investors and advisors using this as their proxy for the idea of the very longest-term reality.

The great credibility of this period isn't just a function of its length (84 years), or of how solid the data are, but of how wildly varied these eight-decades-and-change have been in terms of our economic and political life.

When this period begins, Lindbergh has yet to fly the Atlantic. Shortly thereafter, we experience the greatest stock market bubble and the deepest, longest crash in history, followed by the Great Depression—a crushing economic collapse which brings on the only three back-to-back years of deflation in the twentieth century, 1930 through 1932. (The psychological effects of this harrowing deflation are with us still, as we'll observe in a later chapter.)

We are then plunged into a world war of almost unimaginable violence: 55 million deaths are attributable to it in the six years 1939–1945. It is scarcely over, and the United States established as the only surviving economy in the west, when we must turn and face a hegemonic communist enemy, soon armed with nuclear and then thermonuclear weapons, in an existential struggle for world supremacy that will go on for forty years. Still, we experience the greatest economic expansion of all time in the two decades after World War II, even as we are drawn into two land wars in Asia.

The economy begins to go off the rails in the 1960s, as we suffer the assassinations of a president, of our nation's greatest civil rights leader, and then of the slain president's brother—himself a candidate for president, and the repository of so many people's last hopes. The cities burn.

Oil crises beginning in the 1970s and the long national nightmare of a presidential impeachment give way to a lost decade of stagflation—a hitherto unimaginable confluence of high inflation despite negligible economic growth—and malaise. (Not counting dividends, but considering only stock prices, the equity market in the spring of 1982 is no higher than it was in 1966.) The USSR invades Afghanistan, and our only response is to boycott the Olympics. More than four dozen of our diplomats are held hostage for over a year by a violent theocratic revolution in Iran, and our response is nothing at all. Americans wait endlessly in line to buy gasoline at ten times what it cost ten years earlier. Inflation soars.

But with Ronald Reagan in the White House and Paul Volcker at the Federal Reserve, the back of inflation is broken, technological progress and economic growth reignite as never before, and the greatest bull market in equities—which will last, with one incredibly violent interruption in October 1987, into early 2000—gets under way. Communism fails; the USSR ceases to exist, and a global free-market revolution breaks out. The personal computer brings information technology from mainframe to desktop. And, in the mid-1990s, the Internet ushers in the greatest leap forward in information and communication in all of human history.

Then comes the bursting of the dot.com bubble; the terrorist atrocities of September 11, 2001; long and terrible wars in Iraq and Afghanistan; the subprime mortgage crisis; the virtual collapse of the world banking system, averted only by massive government intervention: the "lost decade" of 2000–2009. Stock prices fall farther than they have since 1929–1932, and then rally more strongly than they have since 1932–1933. Despite torrents of government stimulus, unemployment remains agonizingly high as this period ends.

This, then, is a saga of extremes: of deflation and inflation, war and peace, prosperity and depression, hope and despair. It is thus a period without biases, either positive or negative. It is modern reality. So if any consistent pattern of investment returns emerges from this maelstrom, it deserves our particular attention. And indeed, just such a pattern becomes immediately and quite clearly evident:

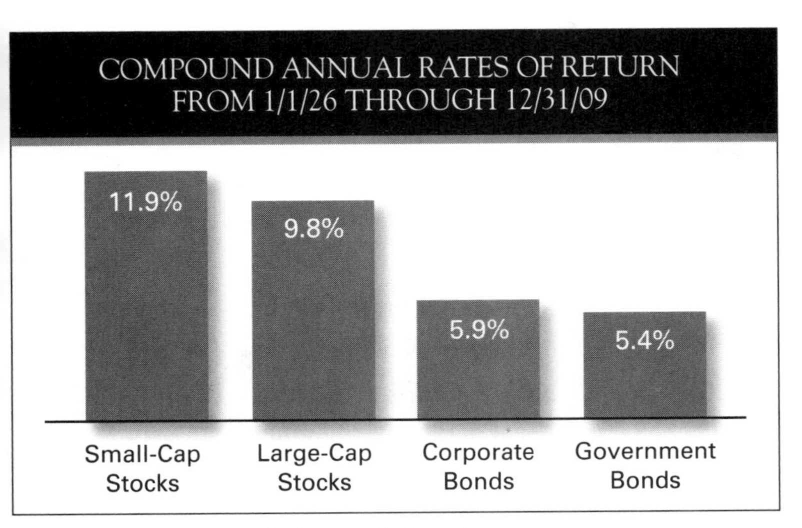

Source: © *2010 Morningstar. All rights reserved. Used with permisson.*

Now, this strikes me as fairly dramatic. It says, broadly speaking, that over this very long, very varied and very meaningful period of time, the owner got paid about twice what the loaner did.

But wait. Those are the *nominal* returns. What about real returns? You see, nominal returns are just the absolute percentage returns you got paid, in a vacuum. The only meaningful measure of long-term return, it seems to me, is the *real* rate you earned: the nominal rate *less inflation*. And the good folks at Ibbotson Associates, who brought you the return figures in the previous chart, also tell us that from 1926 through 2009, inflation as measured by the Consumer Price Index was 3%. So let's back 3% inflation out of the average annual *nominal* returns in the chart on the previous page, and see what those asset classes returned in real terms:

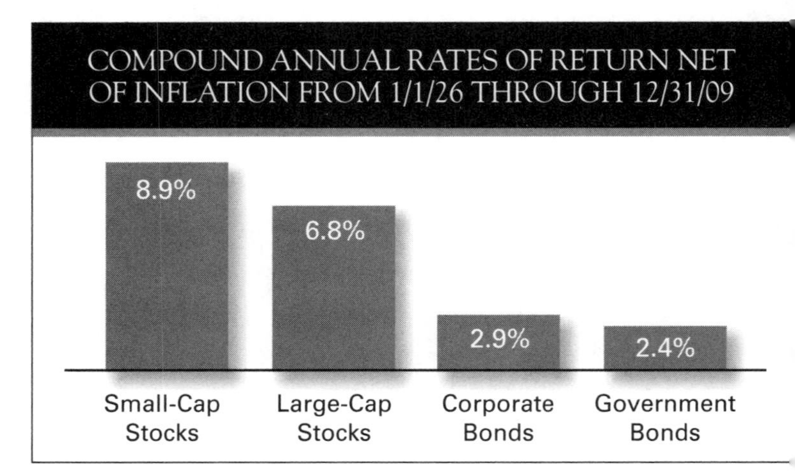

Source: Calculated by The Nick Murray Company, Inc. using data presented in *Stocks, Bonds, Bills and Inflation® 2010 Yearbook.* © 2010 Morningstar. All rights reserved. Used with permisson.

Uh-oh. It's starting to look, in the only terms that really count, as if the owner didn't get paid twice what the loaner did, after all. Net of inflation, he got paid something *closer to three times what the loaner earned.*

Now that's serious. And when you start compounding that equity premium (the incremental real return of stocks over bonds) for long periods of time, the dollar difference it makes gets pretty staggering. Looking at fairly academic measurements of rates of return on a chart in a book is one kind of experience. Watching real wealth building up on your account statements (or, in the case of bonds, watching it not build up) is, I assure you, a completely different kind of experience.

If history is any guide, then, for the long-term seeker of real wealth as we've defined it, bonds are a non-starter. Does this mean you should never own bonds? Of course not. All it means is you shouldn't own bonds and tell yourself you're trying to become wealthy, nor that you're trying to build up your estate for your children and grandchildren. Bonds have their uses; some are financial, most—as we'll see in later chapters—are psychological. Yes, bonds have their uses—it's just that building real wealth over time isn't one of them.

What's that? Still not convinced? All right; I had hoped to spare you this, but now I feel you've brought it on yourself. Let's go back to our historical returns, and factor in taxation.

The most reliable "plug" number I've seen for an average tax rate over this eighty-odd-year period is 28%. See what that does to the real rates of return:

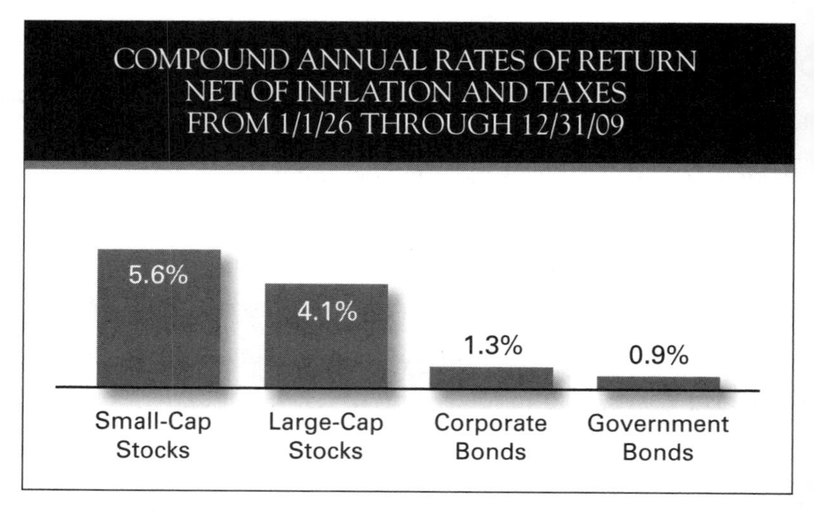

Source: Calculated by The Nick Murray Company, Inc. using data presented in *Stocks, Bonds, Bills and Inflation® 2010 Yearbook*. © 2010 Morningstar. All rights reserved. Used with permisson.

I guess you can look at this, continue the analysis we've been applying up to now, and say that, after inflation and taxes, the owner actually got paid four or five times what the loaner did. That's true, as far as it goes, but I think that at this juncture it misses the real point. Which is that bonds have historically had virtually no net return at all after inflation and taxes. The loaner set the world endurance record for treading water. Real wealth went to, and continues to abide with, the patient, disciplined, long-term owner.

Is this me suggesting that stocks are going to continue to return 10%–12%, bonds 6%, and/or that inflation will stay around 3%? Absolutely not. I have no idea what nominal returns or inflation or interest rates are going to be over the rest of our investing lifetimes. Nor, for the purposes of this discussion, do I think it matters. What I believe in—and what drives one of this book's two central arguments about owning vs. loaning—is that yawning chasm of a spread between the real returns of stocks and bonds. Whatever the equity premium turns out to be in the future—whether it's 2x or 3x or 4x—to the extent that logic and history tell me that the stockholder will continue to earn *multiples* of the bondholder's return, that's what I need to know. And it's very nearly all I need to know.

But there is one other issue, isn't there? And this brings us to the second of the two central arguments about debt vs. equity that I mentioned a moment ago.

You will remember that we agreed, at the beginning of this chapter, that the owners of good businesses get—and deserve to get—a substantially higher return than their lenders receive, for the simple and very compelling reason that the owners take on more risk than do the lenders.

So even I couldn't blame you if you said to me, "Well, the equity premium may be enough to make you a born-again equity zealot, but I'm not there yet. Granted that equities have provided a premium return, but just how much incremental risk do I have to take on in order to get that premium?" This is what I call The Great American Yes, But. As in, "You get much higher returns from stocks." "Yes, but: what about the risk?" This is a fair question. Indeed, it's even a good question. Unfortunately, it's the wrong question.

Remember I said to you, back in the Preface to this book, that people don't find the right answers because they fail to get the questions framed right? Well, we've just stumbled upon a classic example of this—maybe *the* classic example. Once again, the wrong question is, "How much incremental risk do I accept in exchange for the premium return of stocks, and is the premium worth that risk?"

The right question—the *only* right question—is:

WHAT IS RISK?

Just Remember

- All our common sense, and all our life experience, tell us that the owners of good businesses make more money than do their lenders, if only because owners take more risk.

- When you invest in stocks, you're an owner of businesses. When you invest in bonds, you're a lender to businesses. Everything else is commentary.

- Over the incredibly varied 84-year period (1926-2009), which we use as a kind of proxy for the idea of "*really* long-term," real returns to the owner, net of inflation, have been upwards of three times what the loaner got. After inflation *and* taxes...don't ask.

- It is possible that, in the future, return relationships will be very different from what they've been in the past. It doesn't seem probable. And reasonable probability, based on a searching analysis of the past, is about all we've got to go on.

- If in the future the real return of equities will likely continue to be some multiple of that of debt, that's very nearly all the true seeker of long-term wealth needs to know.

- "How much incremental risk do I take on in order to capture equities' premium return?"—The Great American Yes, But—is the wrong question.

- The right question is: **"What is risk?"**

The real key to making money in stocks is not to get scared out of them.

— PETER LYNCH

Chapter Three

WHAT THE REAL RISK ISN'T

The single biggest reason that people fail to achieve wealth in equities—bigger than all the other reasons put together—is that they never really understand risk.

Misperception of risk actually takes two distinct forms. And most investors, without ever realizing that they're doing so, fall victim to both of them.

First, people greatly overestimate the long-term risk of owning stocks. Second, and much more insidious, people seriously underestimate the long-term risk of not owning stocks.

These are not at all two ways of saying the same thing. They're two completely different issues—so much so that this book is now going to give each its own chapter.

This chapter speaks to the first misperception of risk: the fear that owning a diversified portfolio of equities carries with it significant long-term risk of capital loss. It doesn't, which is why this chapter is called "What The Real Risk Isn't."

The next chapter, predictably called "What The Real Risk Is," examines the terrible long-term cost of not owning stocks—of cutting yourself off from their marvelous potential for rising income and growing capital, which are exactly the weapons you'll need to fight decades of increasing living costs during your retirement, and to create a legacy for your children.

For, as you'll see, the great long-term financial risk isn't losing your money. It's outliving your money.

These two chapters complete this book's central investment thesis, begun in the last chapter. Simply stated, this thesis is as follows:

1. The real long-term total return of equities is so much greater than that of bonds that holding bonds is irrational for the true wealth seeker. ("An Owner, Not A Loaner")

2. While stocks are much more volatile than bonds—sometimes horrifically so—the passage of time leaches the risk out of stocks. Moreover, volatility isn't risk, and volatility passes away, while the premium returns of stocks remain. ("What The Real Risk Isn't")

3. The great long-term financial risk isn't loss of principal, but erosion of purchasing power. Stocks increase in value, and raise their dividends, at a much greater rate than inflation saps our purchasing power. The great long-term risk of stocks is, therefore, not owning them. ("What The Real Risk Is")

If and when you can get your mind around these essential premises, the rest of this book will probably make a lot of sense to you. If you can't, it won't. So to the limited extent that

I'm asking you to do any real work, it's in these two chapters. Just thought I ought to warn you.

❧

Before we begin our explanation of what long-term risk is and isn't, let's make sure we've got a shared understanding of what "long term" really means. For the purposes of this book, it's five years and up.

If you have a goal that will require you to liquidate an investment within five years, it's obviously a much more specific—and very different—goal than long-term wealth-building. And you probably shouldn't invest for that goal using common stocks in any form.

Stocks are too volatile over shorter periods for you to be certain of reaching near-term goals. This is not to say you can't earn superior returns in stocks over less than five years. It's simply that you can't rely on such a favorable outcome.

So the more important your under-five-year goal is to you, the less you want to put the achievement of that goal at risk. If you need to be absolutely sure of having a big down payment on a house two years from now, or if your daughter's wedding is coming up next June—if you have *any* goal that requires a very large, specific chunk of capital within five years—I strongly recommend taking a pass on equities.

Will stocks produce a positive return over any five-year period? Probably. Will stocks provide a better return than bonds or CDs over those five years? Still probably, but less so. No matter: when your goal is very time-specific and very dollar-specific—such that you must liquidate the investment within five years—*"probably" just isn't good enough.*

And besides, short-term goals like that are completely outside the scope of this book to begin with. Remember that we're dealing here only with the process of long-term wealth-building as we've defined it: an income that you can't outlive, together with a growing pool of capital that becomes your legacy to those you love. *But that takes time.*

And you've got time—perhaps much more than you think. Your heirs have way more time than that.

So don't go thinking that, if you're 59 and planning to retire at 63, you're within the five-years-no-stocks window. That rule only applies when you'll need your *principal* within five years. A retiree won't. The thing you'll need when you're 63 is twenty-five to thirty years of an income stream that's rising faster than is your cost of living. That, as we'll see, means stocks. And it almost certainly does not mean bonds.

Think—at an absolute minimum—in terms of the rest of your (and your spouse's) life. Then, as soon as you can, start thinking in multigenerational time. Because that's when the force of this book's logic will really begin to come home to you.

✤

While we're nailing down our definitions, let's also make sure we both mean the same thing when we say "stocks."

I'm talking about stocks in the broadest sense: the universe of stocks—the asset class—as opposed to any one company's stock, or even a few stocks. I generally use the S&P 500, which accounts for roughly three quarters of all the value of all the publicly traded stocks in America, as a proxy for the idea of "stocks." (When I refer to some other group of stocks, it will be to make a point about diversification, and I'll tell you clearly what I'm doing, and why.)

Second in importance only to the raw, threshold issue of stocks vs. bonds—of owning vs. loaning—is the issue of getting enough equity diversification—of owning *enough* stocks—so that your personal results can track, and perhaps exceed, the returns of a large index of stocks. (And, of course, broad diversification is one of the great benefits—some would say *the* great benefit—of mutual funds. But I'm getting ahead of myself.)

The fewer stocks you own, the greater are your opportunities to outperform—and to underperform—the market as a whole. Thus, when I make the case that the risk of stocks as an asset class falls sharply over time, I certainly don't suggest that the risk of any one stock does so. Put simply and bluntly, stocks as an asset class can't go to zero, but an individual stock can, and quite often does. (The stock of the airline Pan Am actually did it twice.)

So just focus on the fact that, for the balance of this chapter, "stocks" means the whole asset class. And the risk characteristics we'll discuss are generic to that asset class.

The essential ideas in this chapter are twofold. Or, rather, they are the same idea, alternately traced back into the historical past and then projected into the essentially unknowable future.

This idea is simply that the principal risk of equities—the chance that you will lose money holding them—has historically declined, and ultimately disappeared, with the passage of time. Looking back in time we find that this is no more or less than a statement of historical fact. The chart on the next page illustrates all the one-, three-, five-, ten-, fifteen- and twenty-year periods (starting at the end of each month) from 1926 through 2009, and the percentage of those periods in which the S&P 500, with dividends reinvested, produced a positive return.

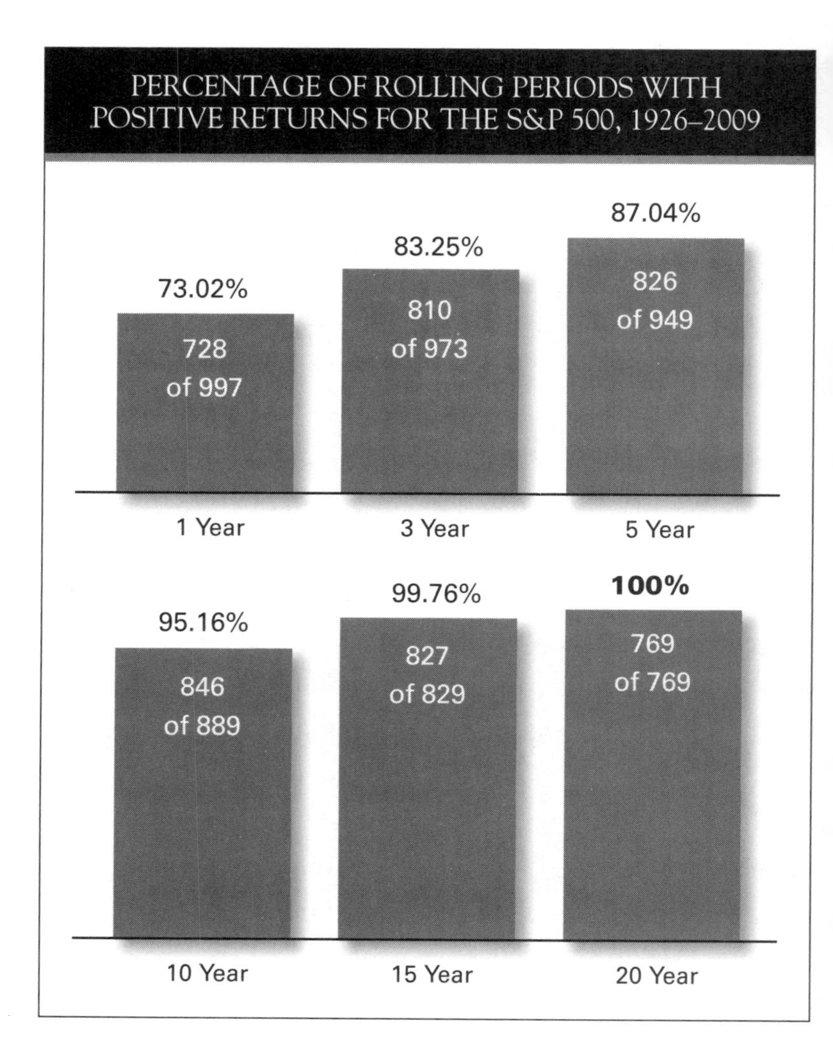

Spend some time on this chart, because it's a testament to the phenomenally curative aspect of the free-market, free-enterprise system. Left to its own devices, the marketplace ultimately heals itself. In bad times, great companies have the resources to stay the course. They have the borrowing power to invest in new plant, equipment and technology. They have the financial flexibility and pricing power to take market share from their weaker competitors, to absorb them, and even to drive them out of business. A free-market economy goes down, in other words. But—and this is critical—*it's never stayed down.*

The natural law of a free economy—and of the value of the thriving companies which shape and are shaped by such an economy—is one of permanent advance punctuated cyclically by temporary decline. It was ever thus. A line drawn between the peaks and valleys of our economic life (and therefore of stock prices) always has a relentless upward bias. Let me say once more, because it's this chapter's mantra: ***the advance is permanent; the declines are temporary.*** Consult everything you know or can learn about history—or, in a pinch, simply consult your own life experience—and you'll find this view borne out.

Not many of us can remember the Great Depression of the 1930s (which was, in essence, The Mother of All Temporary Declines) giving way to the economic boom of the following thirty years. But a lot of us have some memory of the somber 1970s, marked by inflation, Watergate, OPEC, gas lines, war in the Middle East, a bloated corporate culture seemingly incapable of competing with Japan, and the third largest stock market decline of the postwar period, in 1973–74. And many more of us can vividly remember the horror of the greatest

DATES OF MARKET PEAK	DATES OF MARKET TROUGH	% RETURN
05/29/46	06/13/49	–30%
08/02/56	10/22/57	–22
12/12/61	06/26/62	–28
02/09/66	10/07/66	–22
11/29/68	05/26/70	–36
01/11/73	10/03/74	–48
09/21/76	03/06/78	–19
11/28/80	08/12/82	–27
08/25/87	12/24/87	–34
07/16/90	10/11/90	–20
07/17/98	08/31/98	–19
03/24/00	10/09/02	–49
10/09/07	03/09/09	–57

one-day crash in stock prices ever, on October 19, 1987.

The thing that all of those terrible declines have in common is that they are gone: that the economy and the markets have long since overcome them, and gone on to undreamed-of new heights. A day will surely come when we can say the same of the "lost decade" 2000-09. That's how it works.

This is not to suggest that market declines are brief, benign, or much fun. Quite the contrary. When you're watching a third or more of your retirement nest-egg disappearing day by day—

DURATION	MARKET PEAK	MARKET TROUGH
36.5 Months	19.3	13.6
14.5 Months	49.7	39.0
6.5 Months	72.6	52.3
8.0 Months	94.1	73.2
18.0 Months	108.4	69.3
20.5 Months	120.2	62.3
17.5 Months	107.8	86.9
20.5 Months	140.5	102.4
4.0 Months	336.8	223.9
3.0 Months	369.0	295.5
1.5 Months	1186.8	957.3
30.5 Months	1527.5	776.7
17.0 Months	1565.1	676.5

with every media talking head in the country reporting this as an unprecedented crisis in the economic life of America—you wouldn't be human if you did not feel a powerful impulse to sell, and go hide out in CDs for a while. And history tells us that such declines are really quite common. Here's a somewhat arbitrary table of the thirteen bear markets in the S&P 500 since the end of World War II, measuring the market from peak to trough, and ignoring the softening effect of dividends.

I say "arbitrary" because purists will argue that a 20% decline in the index is necessary to turn a "correction" into a true bear market. I count the 1956–7 event simply because it went on for so long—a year and a half from peak to trough. I include the 1998 event because, though brief, it was quite terrifying: Russia defaulted, setting off crashes in emerging markets around the globe, and the largest hedge fund in the world—Long-Term Capital Management—blew up, threatening a genuine financial crisis.

The issue here is neither semantics ("correction" vs. "bear market") nor small percentage differences which do not, after all, change the emotional experience of a major decline. The issue here is **fear**: not what the market is doing, but how you are reacting to what the market is doing.

We know intellectually that the world doesn't end, that the apocalypse *du jour* eventually blows itself out like a hurricane, that the greatness of the human spirit and the genius of free market capitalism must and do ultimately triumph. We know intellectually that the depression ended, that Hitler didn't win, that nuclear winter didn't happen, that communism failed, that Japan, Inc. didn't acquire the U.S. in a hostile takeover, and on and on. We know intellectually that the advance of the free enterprise system is permanent, and that its declines are temporary.

And yet, since 1982, the only four times when equity mutual funds were in net liquidation—when investors as a whole were pulling out more money than they were investing for three months or more—were at or near the market bottoms in 1987, 1990, 1998 and 2002. Then, in 2007 through 2009, we had three straight years of equity fund liquidation. This was the first such sustained incidence of flight from equity funds since 1979 through 1981, just before the greatest bull market in our history. People who had years and years of investing yet to do, who should have welcomed a bear market as a big sale on the quality investments they needed to own more of, instead liquidated their equity mutual funds at panic prices—prices which were almost always never seen again.

How can we square our well-founded intellectual confidence in the future with the get-me-out-at-any-price-before-Armageddon-engulfs-us-all emotional response that characterizes all major market declines? The short answer is that when it comes to investing in general—and equity investing in particular—the intellect isn't in the driver's seat. The emotions are. Specifically, the driving emotion is fear.

It is fundamental to human nature that we fear loss much more than we hope for gain. Or, as Richard Thaler, a University of Chicago economics professor, says, "Losing money feels twice as bad as making money feels good." Let's say I offer to flip a coin, and you can call heads or tails. If I win, I have to pay you $175,000. But if you win, you only have to pay me $100,000. Although we have an equal chance of winning, you stand to gain nearly twice what you're risking.

You won't do it, will you? Why? Because the horror of losing $100,000 on something as frivolous as a coin toss outweighs any rational calculation of how favorable the terms of this bet are to you. (Would you do it for $200,000? $250,000? The answer's still no, isn't it?) Behavioral economists call this phenomenon "asymmetric loss aversion." Call it what you will, the undeniable fact is that we react disproportionately to falling markets as opposed to rising ones. (Bull markets have their own psychological pitfalls, but that's a subject for another chapter.)

Part of the problem, too, is that people have a hard time making the critical distinction between *volatility* and *loss*. To wit, they mistake the former for the latter. I don't usually hear people say, "I've experienced a perfectly normal, temporary 30% decline in my capital in a garden variety, every-five-years-or-so-on-average apocalypse *du jour*/bear market, but that's just volatility, and it'll pass." I hear people say, *"I've lost 30% of my money!"* (With the corollary, spoken or unspoken, "And I'd better get out now before I lose more/a lot more/all of it!")

But what has one actually lost? If the capital isn't going to be withdrawn for at least five years, and if (historically, anyway) five-year holding periods with dividends reinvested have shown a positive return 87% of the time since 1926, wouldn't you be well advised to just ride it out? You would, of course—if fear were susceptible to reason. It rarely if ever is.

The ability to distinguish between volatility and loss is the first casualty of a bear market. When the panic response sets in, it becomes virtually impossible for most people to see that markets may inflict volatility, but—in a well-diversified equity portfolio—only people can create permanent losses. And how does one turn a temporary decline into a permanent loss? By selling, of course.

Let me suggest anecdotally what I mean, by inviting you to look carefully at the following number:

$6,200,000,000.

Yes, that's right, it's six billion two hundred million dollars. A very large sum of money, wouldn't you say? Now what, you ask, does it represent?

It is roughly how much Warren Buffett's personal shareholdings in his Berkshire Hathaway, Inc. declined in value between July 17 and August 31, 1998. And now for the six billion dollar question. During those forty-five days, *how much money did Warren Buffett lose?*

The answer is, of course, that he didn't lose anything. Why? That's simple: he didn't sell. Was this because he knew something intellectually about the future course of the markets that the rest of us either did not or could not know? Did he predict that, as quickly and savagely as the markets had declined, the S&P 500 would turn around and make new highs? I assure you—as Buffett himself would if he were here—that he did not.

Buffett (a) had no need to withdraw his capital, (b) had great faith in his holdings as superior businesses, (c) had equally strong faith in the long-term trends of the world economy, even if the short-run outlook seemed pretty awful, and (d), most importantly, is insusceptible to panic.

And indeed, these largely temperamental (as opposed to analytical) qualities have stood Warren Buffett in very good stead. Why, look how far he's come, as an investor, from the stock market "crash" of October 19, 1987—when he only "lost" $347,000,000! Except he didn't lose anything *that* day either, because...see (a) through (d), above. Indeed, the smile never left his face, and it's easy to see why. Berkshire Hathaway closed on October 19, 1987 at $3,170 a share. On August 31, 1998, it closed at $60,500. And just the other day, I saw it at $120,000.

The best book that's ever been written about stocks as an asset class is *Stocks for the Long Run* by Professor Jeremy J. Siegel of the Wharton School of the University of Pennsylvania. It is an intensive but thoroughly readable analysis of stocks, bonds and inflation from 1802 to the present era. And it offers the most rigorous, most complete intellectual case for stocks vs. bonds you'll ever see. (In that sense, *Stocks for the Long Run* is this book's much smarter big brother.)

In its second edition, the revised and expanded version of this classic book contained a foreword by the legendary economist and investment manager Peter Bernstein, and a new preface by Dr. Siegel. And if you read these closely, you noticed a startling and wonderful thing.

Even as Bernstein and Siegel extolled the analytical rigor of the book's central argument, both men drew the reader's attention to one sentence that appeared in Chapter Five. Indeed, so that there'd be no chance we'd miss it, *both men repeated the sentence*—meaning that it appeared in the book a total of three times.

Now, I've been reading non-fiction books, man and boy, for well over half a century. And I don't ever remember a book—particularly a book as important as *Stocks for the Long Run*—feeling that it needed to say the same sentence three times. So when it happened, I paid very close attention—and hereby invite you to do likewise. The sentence is:

> **"Fear has a greater grasp on human action than does the impressive weight of historical evidence."**

Pause a moment, please, and—if your surroundings permit—read this sentence to yourself again *out loud.* And know that, after all your searching, you've just found the supreme secret of equity investing. It's not holding five-star funds vs. three-star funds; it's not having a faster trading platform than the next investor; it's not even knowing a lot about stocks vs. knowing very little. (In fact, it isn't about knowing, at all.) It is the age-old, never-ending emotional battle between **fear of the future** and **faith in the future**.

If you do not give in to fear, you probably won't sell. Failing to sell, you will remain fully invested in your equity portfolio for the long run. Holding a diversified, high-quality equity portfolio for the long run, you will—simply, inevitably—build real wealth as we've defined it.

The only thing we have to fear is fear itself. No one is asking you not to *feel* the fear, because there are very few of us who ever actually become immune to the emotion. You have to be who you are, and you have to feel what you feel. *You simply have to refuse to act on the feeling.* And that, I believe, is precisely where your financial advisor can and should be of critical help. Simply stated, when your faith in the future fails, she will transfuse her own into you, until the panic passes. If wealth is the product of successful long-term equity investing, and if giving in to fear is by far the greatest obstacle to that success, *then the highest, best and most valuable function of an advisor is simply in prevailing upon you not to lose faith—not to sell.*

I suggested earlier that part of the advisor's value to you is denominated in the saved cost of mistakes he helps you not to make. This contribution, though perhaps not objectively measurable, may, at a critical moment in your investing career, be decisive to the outcome of your family's quest for wealth. In fact, the cyclicality of markets being what it is, and the immutability of human nature being what *it* is, your advisor's intervention may be critical *several times* over an investing lifetime. That's because victory over fear in one bear market may strengthen you for the next, but it certainly doesn't vaccinate you to the point of immunity—especially if, next time out, you encounter a bigger bear.

A skeptic may greet this eternal truth with the response that, since he is never going to sell in fear, here is yet another reason why he doesn't need an advisor. My questions are twofold. (1) Can you be absolutely sure of that? Combat veterans will tell you that, no matter how long and rigorous one's training, you never know how you will respond to the horror of war until the shooting starts. (2) Are you willing to wager your family's lifetime investment success (against an advisor's annual fee of, say, one percent of your assets) that your stoicism is that fireproof? Or might the advisor's fee be better regarded as the annual premium on an insurance policy against lonely panic?

Take all the time you need to ponder these questions, because one fine day your family's financial future will turn on your answers to them. In the meantime, let me leave you with a little footnote on the psychology of fear-based "sell" decisions.

Nobody who sells out of fear admits to himself that that's what he's doing. No one says, "I see clearly—intellectually—that I'm mistaking volatility for risk, that I've fallen victim to that peculiar form of mental illness called pessimism, that I've given in to fear. But I can't stop myself from making this emotional decision which I'm going to regret for the rest of my life."

What really happens when fear takes over is that it immediately dragoons the intellect into ginning up a rationalization for the crazy decision that it—fear—dictates.

Most often the front-line rationalization is current-events-driven. "This awful impeachment crisis (1974), this cancerous inflation (1979–81), this terrible recession (1982), this runaway federal deficit (1984), this insidious Japanese world takeover (1988), this cataclysmic banking crisis and this Gulf war (1990), this terrible recession (1991), this emerging market meltdown (1997–98), this awful impeachment crisis (1998), this cataclysmic banking crisis and this Iraq war (2007), this runaway federal deficit (2010), this will surely be the ruin of us all."

The intellect, which is slowly sinking into the primeval ooze of fear that's flooding its circuits, barely has time to cry out, "But we've had wars/inflation/deficits/banking crises/impeachments before, and we came out even stronger." Then it disappears, totally swamped by fear; its last signal is the four-word death song of the fear-based seller: *"This time it's different."*

Moreover, nobody who's panicking out of equities ever actually says, "I'm never coming back." The rationalization here is, *"I'll get back in when the market is much lower and this unprecedented trouble is finally over."* In reality, by the time the market is down enough—and the apocalypse *du jour* well-publicized enough—for most people to get really scared, most of the trouble is already behind you, and the market's already done most of the declining that it's going to do. (That doesn't necessarily mean it's going to come roaring back anytime soon; it just means that it's already way too late to sell.)

Markets anticipate the economy, and usually change direction well ahead of it. That's why, for example, the stock market normally bottoms out about halfway through a recession. My point is that if you're waiting for a clear, unequivocal sign that the crisis *du jour* is over, you most often turn around and find that the market is long gone on the upside. So the fear-driven seller ends up buying his portfolio back at higher prices...or not at all.

How to avoid all this conflict, anxiety and emotional/financial distress? Easy: **don't sell**. If the market's decline is bothering you that much, stop watching it. (This is a corollary of Murray's Law of Riding the New York City Subway, which states that if you don't make eye contact, you're not really there.) I promise you that, if the price of your home were listed every day in the newspaper, you'd have been scared into selling it two or three times in the last twenty years. But it's not, so you didn't—and look where the price is compared to twenty years ago.

And when nothing can hold back the fear...when you feel yourself being overwhelmed by it...run, do not walk, to an experienced advisor who has seen the bear come and go several times. Because if you haven't sold yet, there's still hope. And it isn't too late to ask for help.

♣

But perhaps you have begun to think about another possible answer to the problem of declining markets. Maybe you're saying, "Why subject myself to the emotional and financial rigors of the bear? Why not just stay in the markets during advancing phases, and get out when the market's about to get (however temporarily) massacred?"

Let me be mercifully brief; this will only hurt for a moment. *It can't be done.* No one has ever been, and no one will ever be, able consistently to call market tops and bottoms.

Please don't take my word for this. Ask Warren Buffett. ("I have never met a man who could forecast the market.") Ask Ben Bernanke, the chairman of the Federal Reserve. ("Don't try to time the market.") Ask Peter Lynch. ("Far more money has been lost by investors preparing for corrections or trying to anticipate corrections than has been lost in the corrections themselves.") Ask your financial advisor, and see if he doesn't warmly confirm the utter folly of trying to get in and out of the market with consistent success. (If, by some perverse chance, a candidate to be your advisor tells you that he *can* time the market, quickly place between yourself and him a mirror, a crucifix, and a clove of garlic. Then run like hell.)

Time in the market, as opposed to *timing* the market, is not *a* way of capturing the long-term returns of equities; it is the only practicable way. You have to stay in it to win it.

And so we see, finally, that as you would be a builder of long-term/multigenerational wealth as we've defined it, you have to buy and hold equities. Buy them, even when every talking head on TV is blathering that the market is "too high," whatever that means. (If you think the market's "too high" now, wait 'til you see it twenty years from now.) Buy them, even when the same talking heads are all crying that "this market's going lower." Buy them, at the only right time to buy them: when you have the money to invest. Buy them, and keep buying them.

Then, hold them. Hold them, no matter how sick the market looks. Hold them, regardless of the economy, or interest rates, or oil prices, or hemlines, or whatever. Hold them, when all about you cry, "This time it's different." Hold them, when fear is a constant taste in your mouth, and every fiber of your being cries, "Get out; get to safety." Hold them, most, when everyone you know is selling them, and telling you to your face that you're crazy to hang on. Hold them, just for one more day. Then tomorrow, hold them for just one more. Hold them for no other reason than that your advisor says hold them, and because you have implicit faith in her advice.

Hold them, finally, because that's the only way to wealth for you and for the generations of the family you love.

Just Remember

- People fatally misperceive risk, in two distinct ways. They overestimate the risk of holding stocks, and underestimate the risk of *not* holding them.

- The long-term risk of stocks to principal historically does not exist. No twenty-year period (with dividends reinvested) since 1926 shows a negative return.

- The world does not end. People just fear that it's ending. In part this is because people fear loss much more than they hope for gain. Therefore they react much more emotionally to declining markets than to rising ones.

- Volatility isn't risk, and temporary decline isn't loss. No panic, no sell. No sell, no lose. Remember your mantra: *six billion two hundred million dollars.*

- "Fear has a greater grasp on human action than does the impressive weight of historical evidence." Jeremy Siegel, *Stocks for the Long Run.*

- The highest, best and most valuable function of your financial advisor may simply be in convincing you not to give in to fear—not to sell. The decision not to sell may one day be the most important investment decision you ever make. Do not assume you'll be able to make it alone.

- No one can time the market. You have to stay in it to win it.

- Buy equities. Hold equities. Everything else is commentary.

It's not what you don't know
that hurts you.
It's what you know
that just ain't so.

—SATCHEL PAIGE

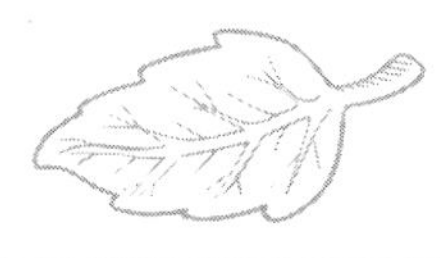

Chapter Four

WHAT THE REAL RISK IS

The real long-term risk of equities is not owning them.

This is the risk that most people totally underestimate. They reason that what you don't own may not help you, but it can't hurt you—simply because you don't own it.

But not owning equities will prove fatal to the achievement of wealth as we've defined it: an income that you cannot outlive, and a growing pool of capital for your heirs. Please note that I didn't say that avoidance of equities *may be harmful* to wealth. The phrase I used—and now use again—is *will prove fatal.*

Turn that idea around, now. Instead of saying "avoidance of equities will prove fatal to wealth," what happens if we say "committing yourself entirely to bonds, CDs and other debt instruments will prove fatal to wealth as we've defined it"? Are these not two ways of expressing the very same truth? You bet they are.

We saw in Chapter Two that, net of inflation, you can't build wealth by investing in debt. What this chapter says is that you can't even *hold* wealth, much less continue to grow it, investing in debt.

Particularly as people approach retirement—when the conventional wisdom says you should switch out of stocks and into bonds for "safety" and "income"—the idea that bonds are hazardous to your wealth is bitterly countercultural. Well, countercultural it may be, and therefore terribly difficult to accept, emotionally. But accept it you must, or—sometime during the thirty years you and/or your spouse are retired—you're probably going to run out of money. If you're both lucky enough to die *before* you run out of money, chances are there'll be relatively little left for your heirs. Assuming that's not what you want to happen, please read this chapter very carefully—and as often as you need to.

Perhaps the best place to start this line of inquiry is with the number in the middle of that last paragraph: thirty years. If, a generation ago, your father retired at 65 and died at 73—which is just what the average man did in those days—you may have a hard time thinking in terms of retiring tomorrow at 62, and (assuming your spouse is also 62) one of you living until 92. But if neither of you smokes, that's what modern actuarial tables tell us is going to happen. (And if you're 52, or 42, or 32, the plot thickens even further, doesn't it?)

Now go back to page 54, and look at the long-term inflation rate, as expressed by the Consumer Price Index. Did you remember that it's 3%? Well, at 3% inflation, compounding for thirty years, consumer prices will rise about two and a half times. Or, if you prefer, your dollar will lose up to 60% of its purchasing power. Either way you express it, you'll need about $2.50 of income in order to purchase what one dollar of income will buy today.

Now, maybe consumer price inflation will be less than 3% over the thirty years that you're retired. Maybe, instead of rising two and a half times, your living costs will only double. Then again, maybe prices will rise more than the trendline 3%. We can't know that in advance. All we can do is consult our life experience and our common sense, both of which tell us that (a) it sure feels like our cost of living goes up all the time in real life, and (b) over long periods of time, it goes up a whole lot. Even low inflation isn't *no* inflation, and when you compound even a low inflation rate over decades of retirement, the results are pretty sobering.

If the foregoing discussion seems like a mathematical/economic abstraction, and it makes your head hurt, see if this doesn't clarify the issue once and for all:

This is a make-believe (except in two important respects) first class United States postage stamp. (The Post Office gets very upset if you copy a real stamp, and since we already had the tree thing going anyway…) The very-much-*not*-make-believe aspect of this illustration is that in 1980, a postage stamp really did cost fifteen cents.

Now, this may not be very scientific, but the postage stamp is sort of my personal bonehead proxy for the insidiousness of inflation in everyday life over long periods of time. And from 1980 to the day you're reading this page is pretty close to the standard-issue two-person retirement life expectancy of people retiring today. (Again, if you're younger than 62, your joint life expectancy is going to be even longer.)

Suppose you'd retired in 1980, and all you needed to buy every year was one postage stamp that cost fifteen cents. And you found that, by investing in bonds and CDs, you could get an income of thirty cents—in other words, *twice* your annual living costs. I'm betting that you'd have felt like you were in the catbird seat, and that no power on earth could have persuaded you to invest in stocks—which were still struggling back from a long period of equity underperformance, and which finished that year at a level of 136 on the S&P 500.

Today, even if your bond/CD income were just where it was in '80 (and of course it's not; interest rates have fallen by more than half since then), your thirty cents in annual interest couldn't buy a first class stamp. You've either figured out a way to cut your living expenses by close to a third—probably slashing your standard of living to the bone—or you're under water. And you've begun eating into principal.

How did that disaster befall a nice, "conservative" retiree like you, who shunned "risky" stocks and stuck with "safe" bonds and CDs? That's easy: you fundamentally misperceived risk (and therefore safety), in not one but two ways. First, you greatly overestimated the risk of holding stocks for the long run. If you'll look back at page 72, you'll see that there've been six bear markets since 1980. And indeed the last ten of those next thirty years produced no net return from equities at all. But the S&P had gone from 136 to about 1100.

Second, and this is the theme of this chapter, you fatally underestimated the risk of not holding stocks for the long run. So, yes, your cost of living rose nearly three times, but your capital would have increased almost tenfold. Much more to the point, even the cash dividend of the S&P 500 went up about four times. Which means that, had you invested in equities for dividend income instead of in bonds for interest income, your cash income would have grown much more than did your living costs. *You'd have stayed far ahead of inflation on your dividends alone, leaving your capital to compound merrily on for your children and grandchildren. And isn't that exactly how we've been defining wealth?*

❧

Why do so many people—heck, why does nearly everybody—get this wrong? The reality of long-term erosion of purchasing power stares back at you, not just every time you stick a postage stamp on a letter, but everywhere you look. The entirety of your own life experience shouts it out to you. And the older you get, the more loudly it shouts.

I paid $3,000 for the top-of-the-line Ford Galaxie 500 in 1968, and $30,000 for a Ford Explorer in 1998. My first apartment in beautiful, historic Brooklyn Heights, New York rented for $185 a month in 1966; not that long ago, one of my daughters paid twice that to rent a monthly parking space in the very same building. (I'm guessing the apartment rents for $2000 a month, at least.) I vividly remember when I was in college—and John F. Kennedy was a president, not an airport—buying a summer suit for $50. I can't find a good dress shirt for $50 today, nor a tie, for that matter.

How many dozens of these examples can you think of from your own life? How clearly is the slow, relentless uptrend in your living costs a part of the reality of your personal experience? And why, when it comes to investing for—and during—retirement, does this most vivid reality get obscured, overshadowed by...something else? What is the hypnotic force that causes even very intelligent retirees to cast aside everything they know about real life, and start intoning, over and over again, "Safety. Income. Yield..."

A part of the answer, I think, is that we are unconsciously assuming something closer to our parents' life expectancies than our own. This is only human: we know what we've seen, and we don't know what we haven't seen yet. There may even be a touch of survivor's guilt in there, as well ("My poor dad barely made it to 72; how can I believe I'm going to see 92?").

The next ingredient in this toxic soup of misapprehension is, as we saw in the last chapter, our much greater fear of loss as opposed to hope for gain—perhaps magnified even further by advancing age. ("If I'm 45 and I run out of bullets, I can go back to work and earn the money to buy more bullets. If I'm 65 and I run out of bullets...I'm out of bullets. The heck with that. Nothing ventured, nothing lost.")

Finally—and most importantly—I'm convinced that the culprit is **culture**, in several of its aspects.

First of all, the defining psychological/economic event of the last century for Americans was the Great Depression of the 1930s. This long, bitter economic contraction is associated in most people's minds with the stock market crash of 1929, the assumption being that the crash caused the depression. It didn't.

This is no time to be arguing reality when the whole issue here is perception, but it was a transcendently awful series of monetary and fiscal policies by the Federal Reserve and the government that caused the stock market event to cascade into a national economic catastrophe. Put another way, the October 1987 "crash" was much greater by any measure than the 1929 event, and could easily have become a worldwide economic disaster *had the Greenspan Fed not done exactly the opposite of what it did in 1929 and thereafter.* Bottom line reality: the crash didn't cause the depression, and we'd never again make exactly the same mistakes that did cause it.

The perception that forms our collective unconscious, however, is of a stock market crash as the root cause of the greatest economic disaster in our history—and of a stock market that didn't recover for years and years. Even aging baby boomers, born much too late to have any personal memory of the depression, were raised by people who'd been scarred and sometimes shattered by it. And those well-meaning people programmed us, almost pre-consciously, with the mantra, "If it happened once, it can happen again. If it can happen again, it *will* happen again." Dad and mom may be gone now, but in the deep recesses of our fear-based unconscious, that tape may still be playing.

Once again, at the risk of appearing to reason with fear, let me interject a few salient but frequently overlooked facts. Between the 1929 crash and the market bottom on July 8, 1932, stock *prices* went down close to 90%. *Dividends went down by only about 50%.* Why? Of course: because companies were not doing anywhere near as badly as their stocks. And here's the best number of all: the Consumer Price Index went down by about 25%. Indeed, 1930–32 was the only period of major deflation in the cost of living in the twentieth century. Those were the years when the vaudeville and radio star Eddie Cantor (who got wiped out in the crash for the same reason everyone else did, and you won't: he was holding stocks using 90% borrowed money) sang, "Potatoes are cheaper, tomatoes are cheaper, now's the time to fall in love"—a joyous hymn to deflation.

Do you not see the beauty of this? In The Mother Of All Temporary Declines, if you were living on your dividends and you didn't panic out of your stocks, your dividend income came down a lot, but so did your cost of living. (OK, not quite as much, so maybe you had to close up the house in Newport for a couple of seasons. But your dividend income and your living costs stayed within some reasonable range of each other.) If you'd invested in bonds, granted your capital held up better, but interest rates went south of 3% for most of the 1930s—and so did your interest income.

By the way, if you weren't living on your dividends, but reinvesting them, this story gets even better. Because dividends held up so much better than stock prices, reinvested dividends bought very large numbers of very low-priced shares. Reinvested bond interest, as you might suspect, didn't buy much of anything, because interest rates were so low. Thus, if you placed half your fortune in stocks and half in bonds the day before the 1929 crash, and reinvested the income, ***it only took about seven years for your stock account to be worth more than your bond account*** ...with the so-called Great Depression still raging on.

OK, OK, I promise: no more reality. We're dealing here with a culture-wide shared perception of the 1929 crash, handed down to us by our parents, and theirs. And what we realize is that the culture has, through the magnifying lens of fear, (a) connected the crash causally to the depression, in a way that it's really not, and (b) greatly underestimated how well stocks really performed (particularly compared to bonds), both as an income-producing investment and as a vehicle for capital accumulation, during those terrible years.

Another important way culture blots out reality is linguistic. Words have tremendous power to shape our perception of the world, particularly when everyone around us assigns the same meaning to those words. If the entire culture has told you all your life that, in retirement, stocks are too risky and bonds are safe, I can hold a 1980 fifteen-cent stamp and a current stamp in front of your eyes for five minutes every hour on the hour for a year. And you're still going to believe—nay, to *know*—that, in retirement, stocks are too risky and bonds are safe. (It takes a village to raise a bad investor.)

Edward Sapir, who did seminal work in linguistics early in the twentieth century, wrote:

> "Human beings...are very much at the mercy of the particular language which has become the medium of expression for their society...The fact of the matter is that the 'real world' is to a large extent built up on the language habits of the group...We see and hear...as we do because the language habits of our community predispose certain choices of interpretation."

I'd like now to examine seven words that American culture uses in very specific ways when it thinks and talks about investing. The combined effect—*not of the seven words, but of what the culture thinks the seven words mean*—explains why people go into thirty years of relentlessly rising living costs with a fixed-income investment strategy...and believe they're being not just rational, but extremely prudent.

The seven words which, like The Shadow of old radio days, have the power to cloud men's minds are (1) "money," (2) "risk" and its opposite (3) "safety," (4) "income" and the related concept (5) "yield," (6) "conservative" and its opposite (7) "speculative." An American pre-retiree might be capable of using all these words within three sentences spoken over thirty seconds, and would believe that he was speaking the plainest imaginable common sense. Observe:

> "As we approach retirement, we can't afford to take the risk of speculative investments like stocks. We need to keep our money safe in conservative investments like bonds and CDs. Besides, we need income, and bonds yield more than stocks."

The speaker of these three sentences will believe in them as passionately as he does in democracy, the flag, baseball and apple pie. And believing (and practicing) these bedrock cultural principles, he's doomed, because none of these words mean what he thinks they mean, and some of them actually mean the opposite. Let's start with the most important word of the seven: "money."

To grasp the point I'm going to make—and to begin to take your own cultural/linguistic temperature on these issues—please reach into your pocket or wallet, and take out one American greenback. Doesn't matter what denomination it is; just haul out one piece of that precious printed paper, and hold it in both of your hands, making heavy eye contact with the dead president (not to slight Ben Franklin or Alexander

Hamilton) pictured thereon. Got it? OK. Now: please tell me what you are holding in your hand, *using only one word.*

I'm willing to bet that the one word you used was *money.* That's your first mistake. Don't worry, it's *everybody*'s first mistake, so powerful is the culture of language. That's the whole point.

The thing you're holding in your hand is *currency.* In no long-term sense is it *money*, if by money we mean a constant, reliable store of value, as in "If I hold on to my money, I'm safe." Currency is a terrific medium of exchange; without it we'd be doing things like bartering oranges for Buicks, which gets pretty cumbersome, especially if the orange grower and the Buick dealer don't speak the same language.

But if, ten or fifteen years into retirement, you go out shopping for oranges (or a Buick) with the same number of units of the currency you've always had, and discover that oranges (or a Buick, or the maintenance on your condo, or a month's supply of your medication) now cost nearly twice as many currency units as they used to, then you learn—vividly but much too late—that currency isn't money. And that, even as you were carefully safeguarding the number of currency units you had, you were (at a compound rate of 3% per year, or whatever) *losing your money.*

You see, in the long run, the only sane definition of "money" is "purchasing power." If my living costs double while my capital, and the interest thereon, remain the same, my purchasing power has halved, and therefore—there is no other rational way to look at it—*I've lost half my money*. (And when my inexorably inflating living costs catch up to and then surpass my fixed income, that's the beginning of the end.)

By the same token, if my living costs double and my dividend income from stocks also doubles, my purchasing power has remained the same, ***so I've preserved my money.***

Where does the fatal cultural mistake of confusing currency with money come from? Well, part of it may be our predisposition to regard the U.S. greenback as extremely stable ("sound as a dollar"), which it certainly is *relative to other currencies*. But that's only saying that other world currencies have historically lost purchasing power at a faster rate than ours has. Sadly, you can't eat (or buy a Buick with) *relative* stability.

In the back of my mind, though, I wonder if this and all other cultural/linguistic roads don't lead back to the depression—which was an anomaly of *deflation*, such that the currency not only held its value but increased in value. (Remember the 25% three-year drop in the CPI?) In that searing period, living costs actually went down, so the value of a dollar went up—i.e. we experienced the opposite of long-term reality. If the depression is as defining as I think it is, that may explain why we unconsciously think currency has some immutable, permanent value—that it is, in other words, money, which it is so clearly not.

As soon as you're able to make the all-important currency/money distinction, one by one the other cultural/linguistic dominos begin to fall. If money is purchasing power, "risk" is that which threatens purchasing power, and "safety" is that which preserves and enhances purchasing power *over time.*

Well, then, since bonds and CDs provide a very small return net of inflation (and since even that small margin is all but wiped out by current income taxation), it becomes difficult to see how they offer true safety—that is, how they safeguard your purchasing power/money. What bonds/CDs are good at—and this will turn out to be the only thing they're any good at, as you'll see when we redefine "income" and "yield"—is stabilizing the number of units of the currency you have at any given time. Sorry, but what good is that, since *currency isn't money*?

Stocks, on the other hand, are exceptionally efficient in preserving—and considerably enhancing—purchasing power. (Moreover, the increasing values of stocks may one day be taxed at capital gains rates, which have historically been much lower than ordinary income tax rates.) We saw on page 53 that, since 1926, the total return of large-company stocks has averaged just under 10% a year, while inflation was 3%—a "margin of safety," if you will, of close to 7% a year. (Jeremy Siegel, in *Stocks for the Long Run*, demonstrates that stocks' real—net of inflation—return has in fact been averaging nearly 7% a year since 1802.) If safety is implicit in the preservation and enhancement of purchasing power (money), stocks are **safer** than bonds/CDs by a decisive margin.

But you give something up—or, more precisely, you trade something off—to get equities' far greater real safety. Being much more volatile than bonds, stocks subject the number of units of the currency you've got at any given time to much wider fluctuations. But again, why does the long-term/multigenerational investor care about that, since *volatility isn't risk* and *currency isn't money*?

At the end of the day, you have a choice to make, and that choice will basically determine whether you run out of money in retirement or endow yourself and your heirs with wealth as we've defined it. The choice is: ***on which end of your investing lifetime do you want your insecurity, so that you can have security on the other end?***

You can have blissful emotional and financial security on *this* end of your remaining lifetime—right here, right now. We'll get you some money market funds, a six-month CD, Treasury bills, and maybe some very high-grade corporate bonds maturing in the next five years. The number of currency units you've got will hardly fluctuate at all. You'll get a little current income, and you'll sleep like a baby. Of course, one day—and that day may not come for twenty years or more—you'll run out of money. Perfect security on this end of your investing lifetime; total insecurity (indeed, disaster) on the other end.

Alternatively, you could elect to take your insecurity on this end by investing in equities. If we get you a little exposure to small-company stocks and emerging markets—which fluctuate more widely, and therefore provide higher long-term returns—we can increase your insecurity on this end even more. The number of units of the currency you've got at any given time will bounce around all over the place, and so may your blood pressure. *Terrific* insecurity on this end...peace, serenity, rising income and capital values far beyond inflation and taxation—wealth, in other words—at the other end.

Safeguard your currency now, risk your money/purchasing power later on. Or risk the number of currency units you have now to safeguard (and continue to increase) your purchasing power/money later on. ***There is no such thing as no risk.*** There's only this choice of what to risk, and when to risk it.

I think you see what risk and safety really mean now, so I hope you'll choose the right risk. When you do, though, you'll be going against your instincts, your acculturation, and the conventional wisdom. That's how you know you're right. If most folks were right, most folks would be wealthy—and, in retirement, would only get wealthier. Since most folks sure aren't wealthy—and since the specter of running out of money stalks many or most of the retirees you know in real life—it should be clear to you that conventional wisdom (about "risk" and "safety," in particular) is anything but.

This is just another reason—if you still needed another—why an advisor whom you trust is going to prove indispensable. For to achieve wealth, you'll have to row upstream against the culture's definitions and rules, and even against your own instincts, for the rest of your life. The comfort and strength of another pair of hands on the oars may, at a critical moment (or *moments*), be what it takes to bring you and your family safely home.

We've just seen that "risk" and "safety" (and their adjectives "risky" and "safe") not only don't mean what you were acculturated to think they mean, they actually mean the opposite, once you define "money" not as currency but as purchasing power. We can therefore quickly—and by exactly the same logic—dispense with the adjectives "conservative" and "speculative."

These two words, as our culture uses them, amplify—or are used interchangeably with—"safe" and "risky." Our linguistic reality-distortion field implies that those investments most likely to limit fluctuation, i.e. to hold nearly constant the number of currency units you own, are "conservative." By the same fatally flawed cultural reasoning, those investments subject to great variability in price (i.e. they can go down a lot in the short to intermediate term, which is what frees them to go up a lot in the long term) are to be regarded as "speculative." I'm hoping you already realize that it's the other way around.

What should a truly conservative investor be laboring to conserve? Why, his money, of course. And what, to the long-term / multigenerational investor, is money? Right again: money is purchasing power. Therefore, those investments are genuinely conservative which most reliably and consistently maintain (and even increase) their owners' purchasing power. *Stocks are conservative.*

What is a speculative investment? I would say it is one which has the possibility of a favorable outcome, but also carries the very real—and not at all unlikely—possibility of an unfavorable result.

Bonds will conserve money (as we now define it for the long run) only if the currency holds or increases its purchasing power. That is, bonds will maintain purchasing power if there's zero inflation, and will increase purchasing power if there's deflation. Judging by the experience of the last hundred years or so, this is more than a speculative posture. It's a *very* long-shot bet.

Even if you do get zero inflation, so that bonds are able to hold the purchasing power of your capital, you're still not going to be happy, for two reasons. First, interest rates are going to totally collapse, because they rise and fall with inflation. So if you're hoping for zero inflation during thirty years of retirement, you'd better start thinking about interest income in the 1%-2% range *if you're lucky*. Be careful what you wish for...

The second reason zero inflation won't make the bond investor happy is that, if history is any guide, you're *still* gonna wish you'd bought equities. Jeremy Siegel found that in the nineteenth century, when technological breakthroughs and massively increasing crop cultivation held U.S. prices virtually constant, stocks still returned 7% a year over (negligible to nonexistent) inflation.

But put these issues of the return *on* your money aside, and let's summarize the point we've been making about the return *of* your money. To wit: if decades of *some* inflation (as opposed to *no* inflation) are probable, and if in the long run money is purchasing power, it is equities which are "conservative" and bonds that are highly "speculative"—just as it's equities that are "safe" and bonds that are "risky."

Finally, we assault the last cultural/linguistic stronghold of misperception: the closely related notions of "income" and "yield." Here, once again, we will have occasion to marvel at the terrible price which fear induces us to pay for near-term (and ultimately illusory) certainty.

The conventional wisdom (*uh-oh*) says that, in addition to their stability and promised return of your capital on a date certain, bonds and CDs usually pay a higher current cash return (in the form of interest) than do stocks (in the form of dividends). And since retirees need to live on the income from their investments, this fact completes the case for the preferability of debt securities. That is, higher current yield is better than lower current yield. The "analysis" stops there. In other words, it takes one component of total return—current cash payout—and makes it the only consideration.

You can't actually do that. (Well, you *can*, but you'll run out of money in retirement and leave your children nothing.) There is no one decisive variable, because everything in investing is a trade-off. If the newly issued twenty-year bonds of a company "yield" 6%, while its stock "yields" only 1.5%, what should that suggest? Simply that, twenty years from now, the income and capital value of the bond will still be the same, but the dividend and the price of the stock may be much, much higher. More current "yield," less potential for increase in value. Less current "yield," more potential for increased value and increased dividend income over decades to come.

The only thing that matters to the rational long-term investor is *total return*. How does anyone manage to hallucinate that an asset class (bonds) whose total return for the last eight decades or so has been about 6% will be a better long-term investment than an asset class (stocks) whose total return has been upwards of 10%? How, you ask? Easy: by completely ignoring the most important (if least certain) component of total return: long-term appreciation (or, in bonds, the absence thereof).

Have you calculated that, as you go into thirty years of retirement, you'll need to draw 5% a year from your investments? Well and good. Now there remains only one important question, and when you ask it *this* way, you suddenly see the toxic illusion of "yield" for what it is:

Do you want to try to draw 5% a year for the next thirty years from an asset class whose total return has historically been 6%? Or do you want to try to draw 5% from an asset class whose total return has been nearly 10%?

For it is, I promise you, just as simple as that. The artificial distinction that people unconsciously make between current cash income and appreciation obscures the one essential truth: *it's all money*. And the only thing that matters is the total return that the money earns, versus how much you're wanting to draw out.

You'd never look at the well in your backyard and say, "I can only safely draw out the water that got in there from snowfall; if I draw out the rainfall, I risk depleting the well." Rainfall, snowfall: *it's all water*. And as long as you draw out less than nature puts in, you'll be fine.

If your plan is to take 5% from an asset class whose total return has been 6%, (a) you've got essentially no margin for error; (b) you'd better pray that inflation doesn't gradually raise your living costs, because your income is stuck, at least for a while; and (c) you'd also better pray that the long-term inflation rate doesn't *fall*, either, because your interest income will eventually drop *below* your living costs, as long-term interest rates follow inflation down. You're between a rock and several very hard places.

On the other hand, if your plan is to draw 5% from an asset class whose total return has averaged about 10%, (a) you've got a considerable going-in margin for error, (b) your income can grow over time as companies raise their dividends, and (c) the rest of your total return—historically close to 5%—can be left alone to compound for your heirs.

Of course, there are going to be years when it neither rains nor snows. In bear markets, your capital will decline significantly, *and* you'll be knocking it down even further with your regular withdrawals. Mightn't that cause you to run out of money? That depends on a lot of things: how much your portfolio had been earning before the bear struck, what percentage you're withdrawing each year, how much the market goes down, and how long it takes to come back.

But if you've built in a sufficient margin for error—withdrawing no more than 5% a year as opposed to 8% or 9%—and if you've hedged your bet by squirreling away a year or two's living expenses in a money market fund, so you can shut your equity withdrawals off altogether for a while if the market gets really ugly, the chances are overwhelming that you'll be fine.

That takes care of the words "income" and "yield," and completes our discussion of the seven deadly words whose cultural/linguistic implications combine to blind us to long-term financial reality. But even after you root these seven imps out of your unconscious, you have to be ever vigilant against further assaults by culture and language. This is especially true when the attack comes via journalism, which (1) always gets financial issues all wrong, (2) always has an agenda but never admits it, and (3) is America's leading producer of groupthink—the conventional wisdom that isn't.

As the economy began to recover from the collapse of 2008–09, there was a spectacular surge in the productivity of the American worker. And productivity is the key to just about everything: our competitiveness in global markets, increasing corporate earnings due to more output for the same wage costs, and/or the ability to raise workers' real wages without impinging on profitability.

But soaring productivity means that, until business *really* booms, companies don't need to hire new workers. Hence, high levels of unemployment will persist for quite a while. This is exactly what happened as the economy slowly recovered in recent years.

Here's the problem: when economic reality contains a positive and a negative (which it almost always does), journalism will devote immeasurably more time and energy to reporting the negative than the positive. Moreover, all journalism—print and electronic—will use the exact same catch phrase to "describe" the alleged negative. Thus: the so-called "jobless recovery," which journalism laments right up to the moment the job market takes off—which it always does, once companies have enough confidence to begin hiring again. *All* cyclical economic recoveries are jobless recoveries—until they're not anymore.

Be very careful of commonly used words and catchphrases. Be especially careful of who's using them to mean what. And be downright scared when everyone is using them to mean the same thing—because that's your cue that they mean something else, and may actually mean the opposite of the conventional interpretation. Above all, be careful of letting journalism do your thinking for you, because journalism ain't your friend.

I *am* your friend, and I conclude this chapter with the same great truth that began it: *the real long-term risk of equities is not owning them.*

Here endeth the lesson.

❦

Should these last three chapters on equities (and particularly this one) be taken, finally, to mean that everyone should always own 100% equities in their long-term (minimum five-year time horizon) portfolios? Of course not. All equity investors—especially those who are retired—should hold meaningful cash reserves, as we'll see in a later chapter.

What I'm suggesting is that there is simply no *rational* case to be made for the inclusion of a large percentage of bonds in a long-term/multigenerational portfolio whose goal is wealth as we've defined it. And therein lies the rub. Because, of course, investing isn't primarily rational.

All investing, and especially equity investing, is first and last a battle with your own anxiety. And bonds, though they may be an irrational long-term investment, do serve as an anxiety-management tool for many people (to the ultimate destruction of their wealth, but there I go being rational again). Bonds should therefore be regarded like any other strong tranquilizing drug: they relieve the symptoms of the emotional disturbance but do not treat the disturbance itself; prolonged habitual use may have very serious negative side effects...and some people are simply unable to cope without them. In that narrow sense, I'm not saying that no one should ever own bonds.

But only in that sense. And, in the long run, it will be far better to treat the underlying disturbance (anxiety manifesting itself as irrational fear of equity volatility) rather than merely to palliate the symptoms. Ultimately, I think that that's one of the most important functions of a gifted, empathetic financial advisor: not to cause some whiz-bang superportfolio to pop out of an electronic box, but to help families find the emotional strength to own what they need to own, instead of what they want to own, especially in retirement.

Just Remember

- Not owning equities, especially during a thirty-year retirement, will prove fatal to wealth as we've defined it.

- If you think that what you don't own can't hurt you, think again.

- A totally fixed-income investment strategy in a rising-cost world is suicide. It may be suicide on the installment plan, but it's still a plan for suicide.

- In the thirty years from 1980, the price of a postage stamp went up close to three times, interest rates from bonds and CDs went down a whole lot, the dividend of the S&P 500 about quadrupled, and the Index itself went up nearly ten times. Which asset class turned out to be "safe," and which was "risky" for the retirement investor?

- Blame it on the culture. It says "money" when all it means is currency, which is no store of value, and whose purchasing power erodes a little every day. The only rational long-term definition of "money" is "purchasing power." And the real risk isn't losing your money. It's outliving it.

- Investments that preserve and even accrete "money" (i.e. purchasing power) over the long term are "safe." Stocks preserve and enhance purchasing power. Stocks are "safe."

- Investments that get ravaged by decades of rising living costs, and are not able to preserve "money" (i.e. purchasing power), are "risky." Bonds and CDs are "risky."

- Ditto "conservative" and "speculative."

- There's no such thing as no risk. Pick which end of your remaining life you want blissful security on; the price is fearsome insecurity on the other. Embrace volatility and anxiety now for wealth later on. Or take comfort in "guaranteed" debt instruments now, and face destitution later on.

- Current "yield" isn't the test of an investment's income-producing potential. Total return is. Rainfall, snowfall: it's all water. Do you want 5% from an asset class whose total long-term return has been about 6%? Or do you want 5% from an asset class whose total long-term return has been close to 10%?

- Beware groupthink in all its cultural/linguistic forms, especially that distilled by journalism. Journalism ain't your friend.

Money, which represents the prose of life, and which is hardly spoken of in parlors without an apology, is, in its effects and laws, as beautiful as roses.

—RALPH WALDO EMERSON

Chapter Five

BEHAVING YOUR WAY TO WEALTH

Equities neither make you wealthy nor keep you wealthy. You have to do those things yourself. You can't, as we've seen, build and hold wealth without equities. But the converse is even more importantly true: *equities can't do it without you.* Your appropriate behavior with respect to equity investments—and not the relative "performance" of those investments—is the variable that will govern your financial success.

And, in the end, your own behavior is the only thing you can ever really control.

Let me string those two ideas together for you in one sentence, so that you can't miss the beauty and wonder of this liberating truth. *The single most important variable in the quest for equity investment success is also the only variable you ultimately control: your own behavior.*

Most people put huge amounts of energy into variables they can't control, and which won't have much if any real effect on their total lifetime return: trying to figure out which way the market's next zig or zag will be, or which large-company growth fund will outperform its peers, to name two. But, as we've observed before—and will again—wealth as we've defined it isn't driven by investment performance but by investor behavior.

In this chapter, we look at four behavioral tactics, to be practiced in different seasons of your investing lifetime, which will have a decisive effect on the quality of your later life and on your legacies to those you love. Indeed, when you take the two basic strategic decisions we've already made—be an owner, not a loaner; never get scared out of equities—and add these four tactical "how-to" behaviors, you've probably accounted for 90% *or more* of your total lifetime return. Which particular mutual funds you select may—I say again *may*—account for the other 10%. But don't be surprised if it's even less than that.

The four behavioral tactics are:

1. setting goals in dollar-specific, date-specific terms,

2. establishing a plan for achieving those goals, assuming a specific rate (or rates) of return,

3. investing the same dollar amounts at regular intervals, so as to harness the power of dollar-cost averaging, and

4. meeting your retirement income needs via systematic withdrawal from your equity mutual fund portfolio.

Like equity investing itself, these behaviors are simple, but far from easy. (If they were easy, most people would be doing them, and most people would be wealthy.) That's why I recommend sharing these plans with your family, so that everyone will become a stakeholder (and a cheerleader), thereby increasing the chances that you'll stay on plan. It's also, of course, why you want an advisor/coach involved: to be the sounding board and the constant voice of belief and encouragement that keeps you plugging away at your plan despite ever-changing fads, fears and "Six Hot Funds To Buy Now" magazine articles.

Just before we plunge into the four behaviors that will—simply, inevitably—translate our newfound equity belief system into wealth, two caveats are necessary. The first is that, before you start a long-term investment program, you need to make certain that your life and income are adequately insured. Your wealth-building program is going to work, provided that you're given enough time to work it. If you're not given that time, or if your income is interrupted by disability, it won't matter how behaviorally disciplined you were. First things first.

The second caveat is that you ought not to begin your equity investing program until your debt situation is under very good control. That means no interest-bearing credit card balances—because, after all, why would you invest in an asset class whose historical return is in the 10%–12% range while servicing 19%–20% credit card debt? All your high-cost debt should be liquidated before you start investing, and I wouldn't mind seeing you pay down a chunk of your home mortgage, either. The classic economic argument that you should hold a 6%–7% mortgage as long as you can invest at 10%–12% is fine, as far as it goes. But since emotions are such a huge factor in equity investing, the incremental peace of mind that comes from reducing debt may, at a critical moment, be priceless.

Behavior #1: Set specific dollar/time goals. What do you want to do, when do you want to do it, and what's it going to cost? A cabin on the lake "someday" isn't a goal. But a retirement income of $50,000 a year over Social Security starting at age 62 and rising 3% a year to offset inflation—that's a goal. Getting to your threshold goal of $50,000 a year over Social Security at age 62 is the part you have to work on right away. And the older you are, the more assiduously you have to work on it.

Now, let's assume that you'll be able to draw 5% a year from your investments (you'll see why when we get to Behavior #4: systematic withdrawal). The question then becomes: of what sum of capital is $50,000 equal to 5%? We divide .05 into $50,000, and get $1,000,000.

So, in this first behavior, we find out exactly how much capital it will take to fund our retirement income goal and keep our income and principal growing. And if you can do those two things for the rest of your life, you can be reasonably sure of "outperforming"—in the only terms that really matter—90% of your American contemporaries.

Quantifying your income goal, and capitalizing it at 5%, gives you one answer (how much capital do you need to retire on) which raises three more questions: (1) how much capital have you got now, (2) how much time do you have to get from where you are now to $1,000,000, and (3) how much money do you need to invest every month from now to your retirement date, at some realistic rate of return, in order to close the gap? These questions are the midwives assisting at the birth of The Plan.

Behavior #2: Make a specific plan for closing the gap. Let's say you just turned 50, want to retire at 62 with the $1,000,000 cited above, and have $240,000 right now. Now assume that you're investing inside an IRA, a 401(k), or some other qualified retirement plan that lets your money compound without current income taxation. (If you're investing personal/taxable money, assume you're willing to bite down hard and pay taxes out of your own pocket rather than from your investments.) Well, at historical rates of return, you're surprisingly close to being done, because at 10% compounded for a dozen years, your $240,000 is going to turn into about $750,000. Now we need only determine what additional sum you must invest in each of the next 144 months—the 12 years until your retirement—such that at the same assumed rate of return you'll accumulate the needed additional quarter million dollars. As you'll quickly see from the table below, it's not all that much, and it may be no more than you were already planning on investing. You're on the downhill side of this thing.

DOLLARS YOU MUST INVEST PER MONTH TO GET TO $100,000 AT RETIREMENT

Assumed Rate of Return	Number of Years to Retirement: 5	10	15	20	25
8%	$1,360.97	$546.61	$288.99	$169.77	$105.15
9%	1,325.84	516.76	264.27	149.73	89.20
10%	1,291.37	488.17	241.27	131.69	75.37
11%	1,257.58	460.83	219.93	115.52	63.45
12%	1,224.44	434.71	200.17	101.09	53.22
13%	1,191.97	409.77	181.91	88.24	44.50
14%	1,160.16	386.00	165.07	76.85	37.09

To the extent that you *haven't* yet achieved significant savings, you've got your work cut out for you, but you've also got a lot of options, among them working for a couple or three more years, and/or taking $40,000 (let's say) rather than the whole $50,000 in the first few years after you do retire. You and your advisor may also elect to take on more exposure to small-cap and emerging markets than you otherwise might have, reasoning that the increased volatility of those styles of investing may produce premium returns...particularly (as we'll see in just a moment) to someone who's investing systematically every month.

And, make no mistake about this, your plan has to be carried out in monthly investments, for psychological even more than for financial reasons. Don't tell yourself you're going to do it in one big chunk out of your annual bonus, because we both know you won't. One year the whole kitchen will have to be remodeled, and one year somebody will offer you the deal of a lifetime on the boat of your dreams, and the days will dwindle down to a precious few...Fahgeddaboudit. It has to be treated like your most important monthly bill. Because, of course, that's exactly what it is.

(By the way, this chart—illustrating as it does the awesome power of compounding—also tells you why younger readers of this book have it knocked. Young people tend to look at the wealth-building glass as at least half empty—they have so little money to invest—when they should be seeing that it's much more than half full: they've got *so much time.*)

OK, so what do you do if you've started a brave and disciplined investing program predicated on a 10% annual return, and three years into the mission you find you've been getting half that? Again, you've got options. The critical issues are (a) that you have a plan, so you can monitor how close to, or far away from, the plan your actual results to date are, and (b) that you take the psychological and financial responsibility for making the plan work—rather than blaming "the market," your mutual fund managers, and/or your investment advisor.

One of your options is to just continue to march, reasoning that, in the great cyclical scheme of things, a period of below-trendline returns will be followed, at some point, by a period of very significant overperformance. This is certainly true, as far as it goes, but the key phrase in the foregoing sentence is "at some point."

From 1966 to 1982, with dividends reinvested, the S&P 500 only returned something like 5% a year (this was the Vietnam/Watergate/OPEC/inflation era, and it featured the biggest bear market, in 1973–74, of the postwar period up to that point). A generation later, in 2000–2009, the net return of equities for ten years was zero, or a tad less. Both these dark periods came after spectacular, multi-year bull markets—as, perhaps another generation hence, will the next such lost decade-or-so. The point is that the average 10%–12% returns (of large and small company equities, respectively) are, after all, just that: averages, which means that reality spends about as much time below them as above them. And neither you nor anyone else can time that reality.

Nothing *may* be the right thing to do if you undershoot in the early years of the plan, but I'd vote for doing something. Most people *will* do something, of course: they'll change mutual funds (if they don't bail out altogether). This is almost always the wrong response, as we'll see when we get to Chapter Six. For the moment, just observe that in switching funds, most people are trying to close the performance gap by manipulating a variable they can't control. Typically, they get out of funds that have underperformed in recent years (and may therefore be cyclically about to do very well) and into funds that have shot the lights out in recent years (and may therefore be about to go cold, particularly if they get huge inflows of "performance"-chasing money that they can't invest well). This may sound like a vicious cycle, but it's actually a downward spiral.

I recommend concentrating on behavioral responses you can control: increasing your monthly investment, planning to work a year or two longer (even if it's only part-time), trimming or at least postponing the start of your withdrawal program. These are actions (or at least planned actions), and when you take action in a constructive, responsible way, good things start to happen. Whereas if you live in *reaction* ("Fund A is underperforming! Maybe switching into Fund B will save me! Or C! Or D!"), you give up control, and compound not your money but your mistakes.

It's not about what markets do. It's not about what your funds do, either absolutely or relative to other funds. It's about what you—aided, especially in the darkest hours, by your advisor/coach—do. And nearly everything you have to do can be summed up as:

Behavior #3: Invest the same amounts monthly, in the same funds, so as to harness the power of dollar-cost averaging. Compounding is only one of two powerful wealth-creating engines which are activated by regular monthly investment. The other is dollar-cost averaging, which completely relieves you of any need to try to "time" markets, sectors or individual funds. Dollar-cost averaging (DCA) does that for you... because you invest consistently every month, giving DCA the chance to do its glorious work. It's heaven's own market timing system for the blissfully clueless.

The principle of DCA is fairly simple. By investing the same dollar amount every month, you buy larger and larger numbers of fund shares when the market declines. You buy, in other words, more and more aggressively as share prices get cheaper and cheaper. When markets rise again, your same dollar investment buys fewer and fewer shares as they become progressively higher priced. Logically, you buy the largest number of shares precisely at panic-induced market bottoms, and the fewest shares at euphoric market tops—which is, of course, exactly the opposite of what most investors do.

THE JOYS OF DOLLAR-C

Month	Investment	NAV	Shares Purchased	Total Sh Own
1	$1,000	$20.00	50.000	50.
2	1,000	19.50	51.282	101.
3	1,000	19.00	52.632	153.
4	1,000	18.50	54.054	207.
5	1,000	18.00	55.556	263.
6	1,000	17.50	57.143	320.
7	1,000	17.00	58.824	379.
8	1,000	16.50	60.606	440.
9	1,000	16.00	62.500	502.
10	1,000	15.50	64.516	567.
11	1,000	15.00	66.667	633.
12	1,000	14.50	68.966	702.

Total Investment $24,000

Shares Owned . . . . 1,426.

Net Asset Value Per Share $20

You end up with a below-average cost, because so many of your fund shares were purchased at relatively low prices and so few were bought at high prices. And below-average costs lead—mathematically, inevitably—to above-average returns. The genius of DCA is that, when you abandon any hope of timing markets/investments and simply toss

AGING IN A BEAR MARKET

th	Investment	NAV	Shares Purchased	Total Shares Owned
	1,000	14.00	71.429	774.173
	1,000	14.50	68.966	843.138
	1,000	15.00	66.667	909.805
	1,000	15.50	64.516	974.321
	1,000	16.00	62.500	1,036.821
	1,000	16.50	60.606	1,097.427
	1,000	17.00	58.824	1,156.250
	1,000	17.50	57.143	1,213.393
	1,000	18.00	55.556	1,268.949
	1,000	18.50	54.054	1,323.003
	1,000	19.00	52.632	1,375.635
	1,000	19.50	51.282	1,426.917
Value		*$20.00*		*1,426.917*

g Value	$28,538.33
Return	0.00%
or Return	17.59% Annualized

in the same number of dollars every month, *your "timing" becomes close to perfect.*

If a verbal description of this wonderful device doesn't do it justice, perhaps an illustration will. In the chart above, I've chosen to illustrate what happens to someone who has what the world would regard as the worst possible "timing:" he starts investing right at the top of the market, which marks the onset of a major, protracted decline.

Our investor starts putting $1000 a month into a fund (which will serve as a proxy for "the market") at its peak price of $20 a share; the fund then declines 30% over the course of a year, which is roughly equal to the average post-WWII bear market. In a second year, the fund/market struggles back to its previous peak, but makes no progress beyond that.

The net effect is that after two years, the fund/market has done nothing; it ends valued at the same $20 it started at. But, of course, the important thing isn't the performance of the fund/market; it's the behavior of the investor—calm, consistent, disciplined, unafraid—which makes all the difference.

Because the investor systematically bought progressively larger numbers of shares as the price declined—and then fewer shares as prices inevitably recovered—his $24,000 invested is now worth over $28,500. He's enjoyed a 17.59% annualized rate of return (because only half his capital was invested at any given time, on average). Moreover, he's accomplished this in a market which—in the rosiest possible view of things—has flatlined. And which, in most people's view, has been to hell and back.

Now, a searing market decline, and a struggling market recovery, are never going to be as neat and logical as this fanciful illustration. Moreover, nothing in this gently undulating picture prepares you for the hysteria with which journalism will be trumpeting the end of economic life as we have known it (and this will go on long after the actual market bottom has passed, so relentless is journalism's effort to find and stress the negatives). But let me not fail to point out that the deeper the market decline, and the slower the recovery, the greater the dollar-cost averager's return will be when prices finally achieve break-even.

You can reality-check DCA by asking your advisor for real-life, real-fund illustrations of how dollar-cost averaging really worked in some of the larger bear markets we looked at on page 72, including (and especially) the so-called "lost decade" of 2000 through 2009. (I suspect you will be stunned.) Fund companies are happy to create any scenario you might want to look at, and when you actually see DCA work—in alleged market "disasters" like 1973–74, the 1987 crash and even the most recent unpleasantness—you'll become a true believer.

Perhaps the niftiest thing about DCA, however, isn't its financial effect but its alteration of an investor's psychology. To wit: DCA makes you love—and long for—bear markets.

On the day that our firstborn daughter Karen Elizabeth graduated from Duke in 1991, her mother Joan (who is much, much smarter than I am, not that that's saying much) turned to me and asked, "What are we going to do with all this extra money?" I suggested that I wasn't aware that we were getting any extra money, and she said she meant the money we weren't going to be spending on Duke. Looking about that beautiful campus, Joan asked, "How much has all this been costing us?" I said, "Tuition, room, board, books, clothes, plane fares and gas for Her Highness's Jeep, about $25,000 a year." Joan said that sounded like about two grand a month, and, with the aid of my $2.99 Sharp EL-233 pocket calculator, I was able to tell her that it was actually $2,083.33.

"Terrific," she said. "How can we make that two-thousand-and-whatever-the-hell-you-said keep disappearing from our checking account every month, and reappearing in an investment instead of in the Duke University bursar's office?"

It was then that I introduced Joan to the wonderfulness of mutual funds' automatic investment plans, where you give them one specimen check and tell 'em what dollar amount to take out of your checking account every month, and they do the rest. "Good," said Joan. "Let's do it." I asked if she cared at all about what funds we chose, and she started to get those tight little lines around her mouth that always appear when she thinks I'm missing the point, which happens quite frequently. "No," she explained.

(Joan apparently thought that the critical issue was whether we actually invested the extra $25,000 a year or let it slip away. Thus, the question of which funds we invested it in must have seemed to her at best secondary, if not actually tertiary. What is one to do with a person like that?)

Unable to restrain myself, I then plunged into an explanation of why that's such a terrific way to invest, because of the way DCA operates. That got her attention. "Oh," she said, *"so what we really want is for the market to get killed for the next couple of years."*

That was exactly right, of course. When you're dollar-cost averaging, you want the stock market to decline the way the Boston Irish used to vote: early and often. In the long run, a bear market is really just a Big Sale, anyway. (October 19, 1987 was the biggest one-day sale on the great companies in America that was ever held in the history of the republic.) So you'd like to give DCA as many opportunities as possible to go running out into a panic-stricken marketplace to buy as many barrelsful of low-priced shares as your monthly investment can pay for.

It is irrational in the extreme for someone who is not finished buying yet to want the market to go up. I can understand someone who's already amassed wealth, and is no longer investing fresh capital, hoping the market will rise. And I can particularly sympathize with someone who'll soon need, for whatever reason, to be a seller; such a person might very well wish the market to go up.

But for the great mass of the rest of us, still accumulating wealth month by month, bear markets (big sales) can't come along too often, or go down too much.

Moreover, the dollar-cost averager thrives on the premium volatility—which is the prerequisite, in an efficient market, to the premium returns—of things like small-cap stocks and emerging markets. The more volatile a sector is—the more it streaks to higher highs and crashes to lower lows around its trendline—the better DCA works. Higher highs mean we buy even fewer thimblesful of high-priced shares at euphoric tops, and lower lows mean we acquire even more barrelsful of panic-priced shares at the bottom of a fire sale. That's why, along with dollar-cost averagers everywhere, I say: I ♥ VOLATILITY. (Come to think of it, that'd make a really cool bumper sticker...)

One caveat. (There's always at least one caveat; neither DCA nor anything else is a panacea.) We dollar-cost average because we have to, not because we want to, since most of us are working our way to wealth and investing some of our earnings each month. But should you receive a lump sum which you need to invest—a legacy, a settlement, a bonus, an IRA rollover—don't dollar-cost average with it. Go ahead and invest it. DCA with a lump sum is a form of closet market-timing, against very long odds.

The stock market in the United States goes up on about 70% of all trading days. (It even closes higher on about 40% of the trading days in a bear market.) Looked at another way, the market goes up nearly four out of every five years. So to take an investible lump sum and say, "I'm going to dollar-cost average in over the next two or three years," may appear to be laudable prudence. In fact, it's a long-shot bet. It says, in effect, "The market's going to decline significantly over the next two to three years; it'll go down deep enough and long enough for me to come out ahead of where I'd be if I just invested it all today." This is market-timing *and* bucking the historical odds, either of which would be enough to make it a major no-no, but both of which together render it financially indefensible.

There may be an *emotional* (i.e. non-rational) defense for dollar-cost averaging with a lump sum: "If I invest it all today and I see it down 30% a year from now, there's a good chance I'll (a) bail out and/or (b) kill myself." This is yet another reason why your advisor/coach was sent into the world: to talk you through deeply felt but ultimately counterproductive non-rational episodes. Remember: it's OK to feel the feeling, it's just not OK to act on the feeling. (Start giving in to your deeply felt but non-rational impulses now, and pretty soon you'll be buying bonds. And we all know where that leads…)

OK, so now we've examined three of the four great behavioral steps to wealth in equities: deciding on a dollar-specific, date-specific goal (or goals); figuring out what monthly investment it will take, at historic rates of return, to get us there; and employing the market-timing genius of dollar-cost averaging to make us consistently smart, opportunistic bargain-hunters, without our having to even think about it. Do these things consistently, and your chances of success—of arriving at retirement (or whatever goal) with the desired pool of assets—are very high.

Now you retire, and it's time for your investments to be paying you instead of the other way around. What's the plan?

Behavior #4: Systematically withdraw no more than 5% of your equity account balance at retirement. Historically, this should leave lots of room for your income, and your heirs' patrimony, to keep on growing. In the last chapter, we formulated the essential retirement income question, "Do you want to take 5% a year from an asset class whose total return has historically been 6%, or do you want to take 5% from an asset class whose total return has been about 10%?" The force of this question is to make you focus on the only thing that matters: long-term total return (as opposed to, among other things, current yield).

The average annual 10% eight-and-a-half-decade total return of the S&P 500 was composed roughly of 3% dividend income (call it snowfall) and 7% appreciation (call it rainfall). And I say again: snowfall, rainfall...*it's all water*. If you are drawing 5% a year out of a well into which nature is pouring anything remotely like 10%, you're going to be fine this year, you're still going to be fine thirty years from now, and your heirs are going to be fine (and will bless your memory) when you're gone.

The only question is: what happens when there's a long drought? I think we all intuitively fear a major bear market in which, by taking withdrawals from a diminishing asset base, we go into a financial tailspin that we can't pull out of, and run out of money. My answer: possible. But, at a maximum of 5%, historically improbable in the extreme.

(Not good enough, you say? You need *absolute certainty*? I've got your absolute certainty, right here. It's called bonds. Live long enough, and you're virtually certain to run out of money. Once again: absolute certainty is not a condition that exists in nature, and there's no such thing as no risk.)

Even in a bear market as bad as that of 2007–2009 (or, more probably, one that you just fear is going to be as bad), there are many options and tactics you can fall back on. The most important one is simply to start into your systematic withdrawal program with a couple of years' living expenses squirreled away in a money market fund. That way, when you feel your anxiety rising in inverse relation to a free-falling market, you can cut back on—or stop altogether—your systematic withdrawal, and live off that emergency fund. (Ask your financial advisor to run some real-life, real-fund examples.)

You may also be able simply to economize for a while, and even reduce your annual withdrawal from the "nice to have" down to the "need to have" level until the rains come again. I'm not suggesting that these fallback positions are especially pretty; I'm also not saying that they'll ever be necessary. The point is simply that if it starts to feel like your plane is tailspinning, you don't have to hold the throttle wide open until you hit the ground. You've got options.

So if your fund portfolio marches merrily along throughout your retirement—providing an income stream for you while continuing to build up your legacy to your children—when do you sell? I hope the answer is already obvious to you: you don't.

Why would you? Isn't the great tree that you planted so long ago still thriving and growing, still offering air and shade and beauty to the people you leave behind? Aren't the great companies in your fund portfolios, and the great managers who run those funds, continuing to grow stronger and smarter and more valuable in a new millennium of globalizing free-market capitalism? Isn't the best, as always, yet to come? Why sell? Leave your children to care for the tree in their own way.

The right time to buy equities is always when you have the money. The only time to sell them is when you need the money. Otherwise...just let 'em grow.

❧

And finally: what if you're already wealthy? Most of this book has been devoted to the process of building wealth you don't yet have, but what if you've got a spouse, three kids, seven grandchildren and twenty million bucks? What if you've achieved all your goals—or inherited from people who achieved all theirs—and your material needs and wants are totally satisfied?

In that case, I recommend the following six-step program. (1) Thank God every day. (2) Bless America, where your fortune is safer than in any country in any era in human history. (3) Ignore Behaviors #1 through #3 in this chapter, because you don't need 'em. You're there already. (4) Follow every other word in this book to the absolute letter. (5) Teach this book to all your children. (6) As they become old enough, teach it to all your grandchildren, because wealth is ultimately the ability to keep the wealth going—and growing.

Then, go paint a picture, or hit some golf balls. Teach your granddaughter to fish. Teach an inner-city kid to read. And don't ever look at the markets again for the rest of your life, if you don't want to...because you don't have to. You're wealthy. And unless a future generation loses this book—or, far worse, loses faith in it—your family will always be wealthy. Simply, inevitably wealthy. Now, go in peace.

Forgive me for repeating myself, but I find I need to close this chapter with the same categorical statement that opened it. Your willingness to embrace the belief system about equity investing which emerges out of Chapters Two through Four, and your discipline in following the lifetime behavioral system in this chapter, will account for at least 90% of your total lifetime return. Everything else, including (and especially) selecting specific funds for your portfolio, will account for the other 10%, tops. Put your time and energy into the variables you can control, and you will—simply, inevitably—achieve and preserve wealth as we've defined it. Put all your effort into the variables you can't control—markets, relative "performance"—and you'll not only drive yourself nuts, you'll be the hare upon whom all the tortoises will have the last laugh.

Just Remember

- Equities don't make people wealthy; people make themselves wealthy. The most important variable in your equity quest is also the only variable you ultimately control: your own behavior.

- Set formal, written goals; make them date-specific and dollar-specific. Exactly how much money will you need, and exactly when will you need it?

- Make a written investment plan for accumulating the capital you need, using historically realistic assumptions of return.

- Invest the same dollar amounts each month in the same investments. That way, even when some of your funds seem to be lagging—and especially when the whole market craters—the genius of dollar-cost averaging is buying you barrelsful of low-priced shares.

- DCA empowers you to experience bear markets as an opportunist rather than a victim.

- A maximum of 5% systematic withdrawal from a 10%–12% asset class (equities) has historically been a formula for an income you don't outlive and a growing patrimony for your children.

- Keep two years' living expenses in a money market fund so you can turn your systematic withdrawal plan off for a couple of years during a major market decline.

- Buy when you have the money. Sell when you need the money. Everything else is market timing, which is another term for madness.

- If you're already wealthy, dispense with Behaviors #1 through #3 in this chapter, and treat the remainder of this book as if it were gospel.

The investor's chief problem – and even his worst enemy – is likely to be himself.

— BENJAMIN GRAHAM

Chapter Six

STEERING CLEAR OF THE BIG MISTAKE

You probably picked this book up thinking that it had to be about identifying superior-performing mutual funds—or at least finding an advisor capable of selecting those top-performing funds, and of moving you into and out of the markets at opportune times.

Instead—with fully three quarters of the book already behind you—what you've found is a testament to the immense power of three essential ideas: ***faith*** (in the future, and in equities, for they are one and the same), ***patience*** and ***discipline***. Above all, I hope you've discovered the primacy of a fourth idea: the absolute indispensability of an empathetic and competent advisor/coach, to buck you up during those inevitable episodes when your faith, patience and discipline are in danger of failing you.

Indeed, if I had to mail you a summary of the first 150 pages of this book on the back of a postcard, it would say:

Dear Wealthseekers:

- Be an owner, not a loaner: a lifetime decision to own equities instead of bonds will govern 90% of your lifetime return.
- Don't panic: the secret to wealth in equities is not getting scared out of them.
- Don't try to time the market: you can't, and you don't need to.
- You can't predict, but you can plan: month in and month out, patience and discipline will be your sword and your shield.
- Don't try to go it alone: hire an advisor/coach whose primary function is to help you be better than you are.

Have a great life!

Your friend,
Nick

P.S. Optimism is the only realism.

Mr & Ms. Everyperson
123 Main Street
Mylittletown, America
USA

So, along about now—in spite of an almost inexpressible sense of relief that so much of real wealth is implicit in that postcard—you may be experiencing two concerns. (Unless, come to think of it, these are two aspects of the same concern.) In no particular order: (1) "Surely he's going to give us some guidelines regarding the selection and management of an actual mutual fund portfolio." (Yes, grudgingly, I am, if only to get it out of the way, so that we can move on to a discussion of the last *really* important lifetime investing issue.) (2) "Surely those few attitudinal/behavioral postcard aphorisms can't be the whole story." (Right again: they're *almost* the whole story, but there is, in fact, *one last really important lifetime investing issue.)*

✤

The text for the sermon which follows is taken from studies conducted by two financial research organizations, Dalbar, Inc. and Lipper:

> **From 1990 through 2009 inclusive—that is, through one of the greatest decades for stocks in history, followed by one of the worst—the average U.S. equity mutual fund produced an average annual return (with dividends and capital gains reinvested) of 8.8%. During the same period, the average equity fund *investor* earned an average annual return of 3.2%.**

But perhaps these statistics are too dry and cold—too abstract—for you. Well and good. Wrap your bearskins more snugly about you, move a little closer to the fire, and refresh your cup of diet mead, while I sing you the saga of the best-performing equity mutual fund of the so-called "lost decade" from 2000 through 2009.

The best-performing equity fund of that dismal decade produced an average annual return, according to Morningstar, of 18.2% per year. This is remarkable enough, surely, when compared to a market that did less than zero. But I cannot resist adding the fact that the second-place finisher returned an average annual 14.8% for the same period. Think of it: that one top-performing fund not only smoked the market, but it left all its competitors eating its dust. Nobody else even got close.

But you must not chide yourself for having missed it. So did literally everyone else, *including—and especially—that fund's average shareholder during those ten blazing years.*

For you see, dear reader, the average shareholder during the decade—based on the fund's critically important *dollar-weighted* return—managed to rack up a loss of 11% per year. That's right: using the average dollar invested in the fund for those ten years (tracking when it came into the fund and when it bailed out) as a proxy for the average shareholder, the real-life average annual return was eleven percent with a minus sign in front of it.

(Lest you think this epic negative achievement mathematically impossible, let me sketch out how it happened. For scale, begin with the knowledge that the fund finished up the decade with about $3.7 billion in assets. Then know that in 2007—the all-time tippy, tippy top of the equity market to date—the fund returned an astounding 80%. Performance-chasing "investors" then poured $2.6 billion into the fund during the ensuing year, *even as the fund went down 48%.* Whereupon most of that hot money—or what was left of it—went screaming back out the door. As the late Zen master Charles Dillon Stengel always said, "You could look it up.")

Stop reading now, dear friend. And, as you slowly recover your breath, ponder the meaning of this starkly horrifying juxtaposition. Because however anecdotally, it confirms the Dalbar/Lipper findings: not just that the average investor underperforms the market, *but that he quite sickeningly underperforms his own investments.*

What explains this? And—equally important—what fails to explain it?

I'm hoping that, by now, you intuitively realize that the universal (and yawning) chasm between *investment* returns and *investor* returns can't be a portfolio management issue. The average fund investor has always gotten a fraction of the return of the average fund—not because he picked the "wrong" big-company growth fund, or because he bought Latin America when he should have bought Asia, or because he thought interest rates would go down, but they went up. "Bad" portfolio selection didn't create this problem; this should almost force you to accept that *"good" portfolio selection won't solve it.*

So if the average fund investor consistently fails to capture an important part of the average fund's return, and the culprit isn't portfolio management...what is it? The answer is that, on at least one occasion during his investing career—and probably far more often than that—the investor makes The Big Mistake: a critical behavioral boo-boo from which his returns can never recover.

In Chapter Five, I dropped the first behavioral shoe: that you could achieve wealth in equities primarily by behaving appropriately—through planned, systematic, patient and disciplined equity fund investing. Herewith, the behavioral other shoe: you can complete the process of achieving quite extraordinary real-life returns by single-mindedly failing to behave inappropriately—by steering clear of The Big Mistake.

(So far in this book, we have considered one incarnation of The Big Mistake—panic—as a stand-in for the idea of the terrible destructiveness of inappropriate behavior. I regret to have to disclose to you now that panic is only one of Eight Great Mistakes, some of which are often made simultaneously, some of which can be made in sequence—e.g. abject panic following upon speculative euphoria—and all of which can be, and usually are, made again and again during the unguided investor's lifetime. We'll return to this critically important issue in a very few pages, after we look briefly at a simple approach to portfolio construction. In the meantime, I just don't want you to assume that, because you now know all about panic from Chapter Three, you've got it knocked.)

❖

We proceed, now, to a mercifully brief digression into the issue of building and maintaining an intelligently diversified equity mutual fund portfolio. Before doing so, let me ritually remind you that "mutual funds" as discussed in this book are a proxy for all managed/pooled investments: separately managed accounts, the sub-accounts of variable annuities and variable universal life insurance contracts, ETFs, and so forth. The issue isn't mutual funds versus any of those other arrangements. (Your advisor/coach will help you make wise decisions among these different approaches.) The issue is: any and all diversified/managed/pooled equity investments ***as opposed to you picking individual stocks.***

But mightn't you do better buying and holding a very carefully selected portfolio of perhaps ten or a dozen truly superb companies? Warren Buffett, the greatest stock-picker of all time, certainly thinks so; he dismisses diversification as "protection against ignorance." Buying and holding just a few stocks would certainly be cheaper than having your portfolio managed. And it'd also probably be more tax-efficient, in that you wouldn't trigger capital gains for decades if you just held on.

My answer is twofold: (1) You're not Warren Buffett, neither am I, and neither is anyone else; (2) even many superb companies stop being superb after a while, and you often won't know this until after the stocks are way down and the lights start going out. A generation ago, a buy-and-hold stock portfolio might have included such blue chip growth stocks as Xerox, Polaroid, Kodak, Control Data and Wang Laboratories. Some of these stocks are trading fairly close to where they were twenty and thirty years ago. And some of them are gone. To everything there is a season...

The plain fact is that a portfolio of a very few stocks gives you tremendous opportunity to outperform *and to underperform* a more broadly diversified, professionally managed approach. And since most of the terrific stocks you're likely to consider are widely and minutely followed by large numbers of research analysts and portfolio managers, you'll still be David, but you'll be up against several dozen (to several hundred) Goliaths at a time.

You're also, I believe, more susceptible to many of the psychological pitfalls of investing when you're stock-picking versus having professional investors working for you. "I really understand this company," "I've gotten to know the management," "My favorite analyst says earnings prospects are still solid," and the like, are the kinds of emotional traps people tend to fall into when they fall in love with—and build big positions in—individual stocks. That doesn't mean that mutual fund investing doesn't have its own plethora of pitfalls. It's just my years telling me (and now you) that most people are somewhat less likely to get their egos and identities tangled up in mutual funds than in particular stocks.

❧

So: back to the issue of a broadly diversified set of managed and/or pooled portfolios—can we just keep calling them mutual funds for the sake of consistency?

Even in the last twenty years, such diverse sectors as small-company stocks, foreign stocks and huge-company stocks have enjoyed long and glorious seasons in the sun. Ideally, I suppose, we'd like to have all our capital in the one sector that's king of the hill at any given moment, and then leap to the next hot sector just before it becomes the top of the pops. This is market timing at its most exquisitely impossible; no one can even begin consistently to do it.

Besides, if we don't have a huge pool of capital to start with, the only way we're ever going to make any real money when a sector goes on a tear is to have been patiently loading up on it, month after month and year after year, while some other sector was grabbing the headlines.

How do you make sure you've got some reasonable exposure to whatever sector is going to be the next big mover, when you can't time sectors? And how do you maximize the chances that you've patiently accumulated a significant position in that sector before it takes off? I'm hoping the answer is already clear to you: (1) diversify across many or most of the major equity sectors, and (2) dollar-cost average by investing the same amount in each sector every month.

Even in generally rising or falling markets, some sectors will usually be performing better than others. Moreover, overseas markets may behave very differently from the U.S. market, and even from each other, as much because the currencies are moving in different directions as because of economic fundamentals. Broad equity diversification, therefore, can capture the long-term returns of the different equity sectors. And it will usually (though not always) mute, to some extent, the overall volatility of your portfolio, since all your sectors won't usually be soaring or cratering in unison. Small-cap vs. large-cap, international vs. domestic U.S., growth stocks vs. value stocks: they all tend to run on somewhat different cycles, though the timing of those cycles can't be predicted.

That logic leads me to a very basic portfolio that has five mutual funds in it, each representing a very different sector or investment style:

We know that growth and value tend to move countercyclically to each other, and end up in about the same place in terms of overall long-term return. (From time to time you will run across arguments that growth permanently outperforms value or vice versa. Ignore them.) We know, too, that big-cap and small-cap stocks usually dance a contrapuntal minuet; the latter does indeed produce a higher long-term return (with, and because of, higher volatility).

Finally, we know that foreign markets do their own things at their own times, often (though not always) irrespective of

U.S. markets. So international/emerging market investing—in addition to putting you on the front lines of the global capitalist revolution—can raise your overall portfolio return while potentially reducing your overall portfolio volatility. (Emerging markets *themselves* are, of course, way more volatile than ours—anybody remember some of the Asian markets halving in a matter of weeks in 1998? So remember: it's only lower *portfolio* volatility we're talking about, here.)

Could you take this elegant, simple five-part portfolio and diversify it even further? Well, sure you could—although I'm not sure the incremental gain would be worth the trouble. You could, for instance, divide your international exposure into a number of more specific sub-categories: Europe, Asia and Latin America, for instance, or mature markets and emerging ones, or big-cap and small-cap. But up around seven to nine different funds/accounts, I think you're at the point of ceasing to be an investor; you're turning into a collector. And north of ten funds, you're so diversified that what you actually own is one huge, very inefficient and terribly expensive index fund.

❧

And that's probably my cue to step out of the logic of equity diversification for another moment, and review the issues surrounding indexing, also known as passive investing.

An index—any index, be it the S&P 500, the NASDAQ Composite, the Russell 2000 or even the Wilshire 5000—tells you the average return of all the money that's invested in all the stocks in that index. In other words, any index starts out as a 50th percentile performer. Half the dollars invested get a higher return, and half of them get a lower return.

But you and I can't buy an index; the closest we can come is to buy an index *fund*, which should give us the index return *less the expenses of running the fund*. Happily, index fund expenses should be pretty low. There are no research or other active management costs, just the mostly mechanical expenses of keeping the fund's portfolio as nearly identical to the index as possible, plus legal and accounting expenses, mailings and distributions to shareholders, and some small profit for the fund's sponsor. Vanguard Index 500 Fund, the largest of the S&P 500 Index funds (and the one whose management is most publicly hawkish about keeping costs low), has averaged less than 0.30% in annual expenses (three-tenths of one percent, or—in the jargon—thirty basis points).

The fund's actively managed peers, often called large-cap blend funds (because they own big-company stocks in both the growth and value categories) probably averaged one full percentage point more—say a total of 1.30%—in research, trading and other costs associated with the effort to provide performance superior to that of the index. And therein lies the crux of the argument.

The indexers say that the incremental costs of active management aren't worth it. They hold that the market is so efficient that active research won't be able consistently to select enough stocks that are priced so wrong (relative to the other stocks in the index) that they'll return more than the index plus the incremental management costs.

Indexers—the rational ones, at least—do *not* suggest that active managers can't beat an index fund. Indeed, a fair estimate is that—again, given the higher costs of active management—an S&P 500 Index fund should perhaps beat 60%–65% of the money that's invested in its peer group of funds. But, contend the indexers, the third-or-so of active mangers who do beat an index fund can't be identified in advance. Ten years into his tenure at Magellan Fund, Peter Lynch had a superb record. But you couldn't know for sure whether Lynch or Joe Blow from Kokomo—or neither, or both—would beat the S&P in the next block of time, because there's no statistical evidence for the persistence of performance in equity mutual funds.

These arguments make my eyes glaze over. First of all, as I've said all along, wealth isn't driven by the relative performance of investments, but by the absolute behavior of investors. When CNBC's ace market commentator Chicken Little comes on and says that the sky is falling, are you any less likely to bail out of an index fund than an actively managed fund when they're both down 30%? Do you need the behavioral coaching of a gifted advisor any less because you're indexing?

Remember: all we're doing in this chapter is slicing and dicing the last 10% or so of your total lifetime return, since the first 90%—governed entirely by the beliefs and behaviors prescribed in earlier chapters—is already in the barn. (Or it's not, because you didn't buy into the previous chapters—in which case putting a lot of energy into the issue of indexing vs. active management will be akin to rearranging the deck chairs on the *Titanic.*)

Moreover, all indexes aren't created equal. The market for the 500 largest publicly held companies may be so deep and liquid, and the research capabilities brought to bear on those 500 stocks so ferocious, that it's relatively hard to pick stocks that are mispriced relative to the index. But this is surely not the case in smaller, shallower, less efficient markets where research coverage is much more hit-and-miss (the small-cap arena, for example) or where the quality of financial disclosure itself is spottier (as is the case in many emerging markets). In such situations, active management (stock picking) can yield significant rewards.

But even that's somewhat beside the point. Which is, of course, that the issue isn't really active vs. passive investing. *The issue is cost.* There are some surprisingly high-expense-ratio index funds out there. Perhaps more to the point, there are lots of actively managed funds that follow a long-term, buy-and-hold, low-turnover investment strategy, and which therefore have relatively low expenses. And these, I believe, are the kinds of actively managed funds long-term investors like us should be looking at.

So, let's leave it at this: (1) Indexing is one sensible approach to portfolio management; it's not a panacea. (2) If you and your advisor decide to make an S&P 500 Index fund a core holding, and build a portfolio of actively managed funds around it, that's fine. (3) But trying to index all five of the basic sectors/styles I suggested on page 162 may not be smart. It obviously won't get you killed, but it may—particularly in small-cap and emerging markets—cause you to leave some significant money on the table that you really needn't leave there. (4) Be guided by the advisor you've elected to trust on this and indeed all other portfolio issues. (5) *Active/passive can't ever be the make-or-break issue in long-term, real-life return.*

❦

OK, now back to our continuing discussion of building an equity fund portfolio for all the seasons of your life. So far we know that we're going to have a relatively few funds—say five, one from each of the major sectors/styles of equities. One cautionary note: make sure you're really diversifying by sector/style, not just by the stated investment objective of the fund. For example, here's a "portfolio" of five funds diversified by investment objective:

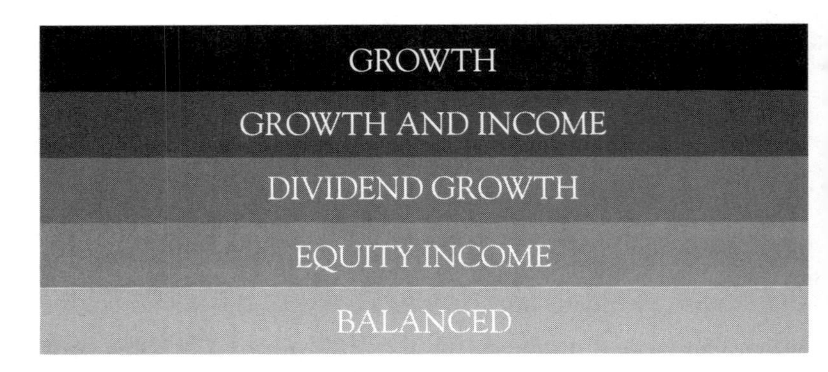

At first glance, that may seem like a whole lot of diversification. But then you'll look at the top ten stock holdings in the five funds, and find out they've all got Pepsi or Coke, Merck or Pfizer, Disney or Comcast, Bank of America or JPMorgan Chase, and McDonald's or McDonald's (!). From the standpoint of diversification, this is like eating a balanced diet of white bread, rye bread, whole wheat bread, pumpernickel bread and a sesame seed bagel. A "portfolio" like that will probably soar and dive in tighter formation than the Blue Angels!

Now, since you probably don't need me to tell you how to pick index funds, let's talk about how to select actively managed funds. First, though—and this is critical—let's make sure we completely understand the most important way *not* to pick funds: short-term (five years or less) "performance."

A subtle way to look at the phenomenon of how short-term performance-chasing always sends you the wrong signal is a study from Davis Advisors. The good folks at Davis looked at a universe of 176 large-cap managers (growth and value) whose 10-year annualized performance ranked in the top quartile—again, the best 25%—for the ten years through December 31, 2009.

Then they asked: what percentage of those longer-term top performers had at least one rolling three-year period during which they went completely off the rails, putting up numbers somewhere between mediocre and downright terrible?

Specifically, what percentage of these star managers had at least a three-year run when they were in the bottom half of all their large-cap peers, what percentage ran at least three years in the bottom quartile...and what percentage (if any!) put together a three-year streak so atrocious that it landed them in the bottom decile...the worst ten percent for those three years?

The results cannot fail to startle you: just about all these long-term winners (96%) underperformed at least half their peers over a three-year run. More than three quarters of them (79%) occupied the bottom quartile for at least three years running. And—get this—very nearly half (47%) of the big-cap managers who were in the top quartile for the ten years through 2009 spent at least three solid years in the doghouse—being outperformed by 90% of their peers over that period! Thus, the very worst portfolio strategy you can ever adopt is: buying managers when they're hot…and switching out of them when they're not.

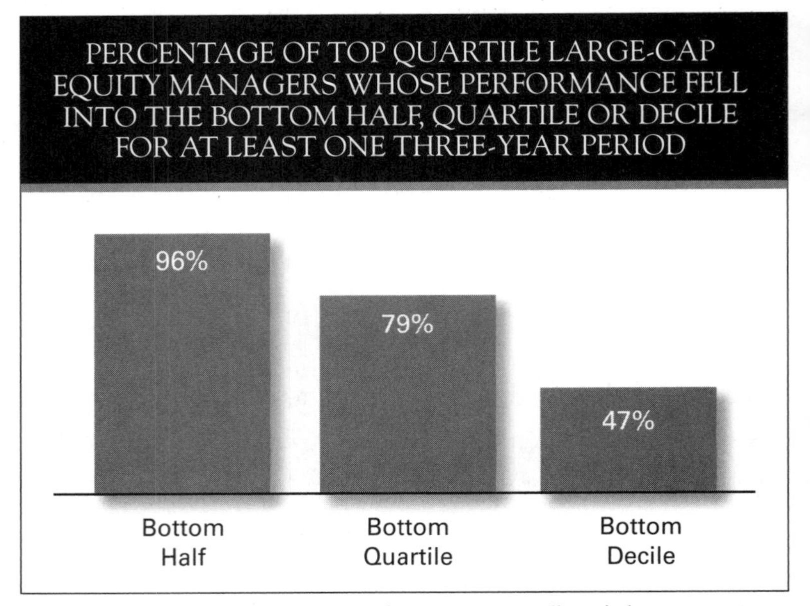

Source: Davis Advisors. 176 managers from eVestment Alliance's large-cap universe whose 10-year average annualized performance ranked in the top quartile from January 1, 2000–December 31, 2009.

Once again, if these somewhat dry statistics don't quite do it for you, let me sing you one more saga. This one concerns the epic hero who—right through the middle of the "lost decade"—ran off a streak of fifteen straight years of outperforming the S&P 500. Not only had this feat never been accomplished before, but *the manager himself—blessings and peace be upon him—tried desperately to communicate to anyone who would listen* ***that he wasn't really doing it!*** In his fourth quarter 2005 letter, he pointed out that he had only beaten the S&P fifteen years running *measured to December 31.* And that if you looked at all the fifteen-year periods ending in any other month, he hadn't.

No one would listen. The performance-chasing lemmings poured in. And sure enough, in very short order the manager put together three years in a row when he was in **the bottom one percent of all the funds in his peer group.**

Chasing recent past "performance" is investing in a rear-view mirror, and it's as close as you'll ever get to a guarantee of underperformance. This is simply because meteoric runs by sectors/styles are finite, and because whoever/whatever shot the lights out in the last five years is a pretty good candidate to go into hibernation—just when "performance" junkies, incited by "Six Hot Funds To Buy Now!" journalism, are coming in through the doors and the windows, up the cellar staircase and down the chimney.

OK, so what should you and your advisor be looking for, if you're going to seek active management? Well, first and foremost, I think you should look for managers who have a significant body of experience. Yes, I know—in some cold, distant, mathematical way—that there's no *overall* statistical evidence for the persistence of performance. But I also know that Buffett tends to continue to be Buffett, Lynch to be Lynch, and John Templeton to be John Templeton—until they retire or die. Genuinely good, smart people (and those two attributes are not the same thing) tend, if anything, to get better and smarter. They also tend to be disciplined (and humble) enough to stick to what they're good at, and you need your managers to stay disciplined if you're going to stay diversified. That means sticking to their knitting even—and especially—when their style of knitting is out of vogue. You don't want to wake up one morning and find out that all five of your managers own the Nifty Fifty growth stocks.

I like managers who've been running their funds for a good long time, so that the longer-term record of the fund actually tells you something useful about the manager. (That means I don't follow managers who change jobs a lot, nor funds that change managers a lot.) I don't look for managers who are necessarily outperforming "the market," but I do want to see that, in the long run, the manager is doing better than most of his peers, i.e. funds that own the same kinds of stocks.

Ideally, your advisor should know that manager personally (or at least his firm should) and ultimately so should you. Even the most quantitative advisors I know—who rely chiefly on very rigorous, higher-mathematical screening methods—spend a fair amount of time eyeball-to-eyeball with their managers, probing for intellectual and emotional consistency. And you may very well want to become part of that process at some point, if only for the incremental comfort of knowing the people to whom you've consigned your family's hopes for wealth. (I once took my children's mother to see a money manager who I thought was the bee's knees. She thought he was as phony as the proverbial three dollar bill. As so often happens, she turned out to be right. I'm not sure what that tells you, but I did seem to feel the need to share it with you, as part of my therapy.)

Beyond that, the big thing I look for is low turnover. I'm a long-term buy-and-holder, and that's what I want from my managers. (Buffett: "Our favorite holding period is forever.") Consistently high turnover tells me that the manager is trading stocks rather than investing in them, and/or trying to call short-term turns in the market. These are two things I don't believe anyone can consistently do well, and I don't want anyone trying to do them with my money. You shouldn't either.

Low turnover is, to me, almost a character trait, and it usually leads to a low expense ratio as well as more tax efficiency. I haven't said much about taxes yet—and after this paragraph I'm not going to say anything else at all—because taxes should always be the tail, never the dog. Everything else being equal,

I'd certainly rather pay taxes later (at long-term capital gains rates, one hopes) than sooner. And a low-turnover, buy-and-hold management style plays to that preference. But you should never make an investment decision primarily based on taxes. Second only to short-term performance, taxes are the dumbest variable you can isolate on.

If you follow these guidelines, won't you screen out the 35-year-old next Peter Lynch, because he doesn't have a record? Sure you will—and a couple of dozen 35-year-old palookas who aren't going anywhere but to Palookaville. Won't you screen out someone who apprenticed at a big fund company, got a lot of experience managing two or three different funds in turn, and is just now starting a new fund, all on his own, that's going to be great? Yes, and you'll screen out mediocrities who are starting their own funds because they became unemployable anywhere else. This isn't science, and I'm not a scientist.

I just said: if you're seriously committed to achieving wealth, are trying to filter out the unbearable cacophony of fund advertising and journalism, and are looking for criteria that will help you find managers of demonstrated competence and character, start with these. (If your advisor has other criteria that both you and she agree might be more appropriate for you, start with those. Just (a) have a consistent, disciplined approach to fund selection—don't dither about it—and (b) get going.)

And, before you know it, you'll be dollar-cost averaging every month into five equity funds with experienced, disciplined, successful managers who invest for the long term, don't turn their portfolios over too much, and therefore keep their expense ratios pretty low. You're on your way.

Select your five funds as if they were all going to be in your estate. Invest 20% equally in each of the five—otherwise, even though you may not admit it, you're making market predictions. And you're probably going to make the wrong prediction (a) because we all do, but particularly (b) because, left to your own devices, you're going to be staring into that old rear-view mirror. ("I think I'll put 30% in big-cap and 10% in small-cap, instead of 20% and 20%, because big-cap has been doing so much better these last four years." *Clang!*)

Having built your five-pointed shining star of a portfolio, your next temptation—which will never stop coming back while life and breath remain in you—will be to tweak it. "Tweak," in this context, is a very precise, technical investment term which translates, "Tear off one of its legs and try to beat the portfolio to death with it."

You see, if the portfolio is properly diversified, some of its components will be shooting the lights out while others are lying there, bleeding quietly into the carpet. Then, without warning, they'll do a role reversal. This is a good thing.

First, it means you're truly well-diversified, so that you're going to get the long-term returns of all your equity components, but the overall portfolio will enjoy somewhat reduced volatility. (Because its sectors/styles are running on different cycles, as we saw earlier, the entire portfolio will tend not to soar and crash in formation.)

Second, and potentially even more important, your dollar-cost averaging program will be systematically buying barrelsful of the laggard(s) while reluctantly acquiring thimblesful of whatever's flying. No one ever got wealthy paying top dollar; most seriously monied people got that way buying things that were distressed, out of favor, and therefore on sale. DCA is the *ultimate* smart shopper.

So leave it alone. Do not—as most Americans do, soon or late (or both)—sell the thing that's on sale to buy the thing whose price just got marked up a whole lot. Because that's a formula for owning things that soared in value *before* you bought 'em, and dumping things that soar in value (relatively) soon *after* you sell 'em. And *that's* a formula for becoming a very, very sad, bad, underachieving investor.

Dollar-cost averaging is the best portfolio manager the world has ever known. And it will work perfectly...unless you reach in and try to "help" it—which, I say again, will be a constant temptation. And so I leave you with this Zen question: how many multiples of her 1%-or-so-a-year fee is your advisor worth *if she can just talk you into doing nothing for the next 30 years?* Because, once you have your properly diversified fund portfolio in place, and once you're dollar-cost averaging evenly into its five components each month...nothing will be the rarest and the most valuable thing that you can do. But without help, you may find it impossible—as most people do, which is why most people ain't wealthy.

Yes, but...in the real world, some of your portfolio managers are going to leave and go elsewhere, some are going to retire (Peter Lynch did), and some are going to die (John Templeton did). So be it. Then you have some decisions to make. Fortunately, in the person of your advisor, you have a friend and a coach and an empathetic counselor to help you make those decisions.

If a very good manager whose work you've come to respect and rely on goes elsewhere, my bias would be to follow him/her. Ideally, I'd try to get on a conference call with the old manager who's moved on, and another call with the new manager of the old fund. I'd also probably look at a couple of other good funds in the same sector/style. Then I'd consult my advisor's head and my own tummy, if you take my meaning, and make a decision.

If the manager has gone completely off the landscape, I'd again want to hear what the new manager(s) had to say. But I'd also ask my advisor, "If the late lamented manager was king/queen of this style, who are the crown princes/princesses?" Just remember: this isn't a science, and the new person you're about to pick to run 20% of your portfolio cannot, in the great scheme of things, be critical to the success or failure of your overall long-term/multigenerational wealth-building program. *Only you can be that.*

I hope that, so far, this chapter has finally convinced you that there is no way for you and your advisor to pick actively managed mutual funds which consistently "outperform" the huge preponderance of your neighbors' mutual funds. Now, to conclude this chapter's (and, indeed, this whole book's) central argument, let me confirm to you an infinitely greater truth: that you—with your advisor/coach's indispensable behavioral guidance—are probably going to get a better real-life financial outcome than are the great bulk of your neighbors.

Understanding that these are two entirely different and totally unrelated outcomes is the beginning of all wisdom. *Inappropriate behavior is the ultimate disconnect.* Throw the monkey wrench of The Big Mistake into the works of a superior mutual fund portfolio, and the real-life financial outcome—the *investor* return, as opposed to the *investment* return—is going to be a train wreck.

And a disciplined, diversified portfolio of even the most ordinary equity funds which simply fails to get derailed by The Big

Mistake will provide a relatively superior real-life outcome.

What, then, are the Eight Great Mistakes? How might we immunize ourselves against them? Or what serums will our advisor/coach ask permission to inject us with when the fever of one (or more) of the Eight Great Mistakes threatens to break out?

In no particular order of importance or danger, the Eight Great Mistakes are:

☠ OVERDIVERSIFICATION

You invest in your five core funds. Then you read an utterly fascinating article about another...so you put some money in it. Then a red hot manager starts her own new fund, so you buy some of that, too. And again. And again...

Bingo: one fine day you look around, as we observed earlier in this chapter, and you're not an investor anymore, you're a collector. And you haven't got a portfolio; it's more like a bric-a-brac shelf. Too late, you realize that, when you own just about everything, you don't really own anything.

The antidote is to accept that the grass is not, in fact, greener on the other side of the street. In practice, assume you were only issued five mutual fund chits for your whole lifetime, and that you've spent them all. So to buy a new fund, you have to sell one of the five you already own. Then remember that the fund you want to deep-six probably hasn't "stopped working" permanently; that manager is usually just out of sync with the market—and every day is getting you closer to his turn in the cycle.

At that point, don't just do something. Stand there.

☠ UNDERDIVERSIFICATION

This is really a bad one, because it feels so logical while it's setting you up for the kill. Underdiversification manifests itself as the impulse to keep narrowing your portfolio down to "what's working." The trouble is that, particularly as markets approach significant tops, the universe of "what's working" shrinks down, ultimately to one idea.

In 1999, I heard a lot of people insisting that they were still diversified, because they had holdings in tech *and* telecom *and* dot.com. Trouble was that all three of these "industries" were premised, by then, on one hypothesis: the continued exponential growth of the Internet.

Underdiversification—the fatal narrowing of a portfolio down to essentially one idea—pretty much assures that you'll be in the last thing that's "working" *just before all the lights go out.* In 2000–2002, when the broad market declined 50%, NASDAQ's tech-heavy index fell 80%.

By 2010, after a decade of no returns from equities, portfolios contained 100% bonds/cash and no stocks. Classic underdiversification: the fatal narrowing of the portfolio down to the one idea of Armageddon. (The lunatic fringe of Armageddon seekers didn't even trust bonds and cash: they were underdiversified in gold.)

Another insidious form of underdiversification is having too much of your invested net worth in just one stock—either because you inherited it, or because you worked for a company and bought its stock for 30 years, or whatever. Here in the real world, we live by the iron law of what the great economist Joseph Schumpeter called "creative destruction." In plain English, that means that you can get wealthy by underdiversifying, but you can't stay wealthy by underdiversifying. Generations of brokenhearted undiversified stockholders in yesterday's blue chips—the Sears Roebucks, the Kmarts, the Johns Manvilles, the Kodaks, the Polaroids, the Penn Central Railroads—will tell you: no matter how blue it may be right now, no blue chip is indefinitely exempted from the law of creative destruction. Having a hugely disproportionate percentage of your wealth in one stock isn't even investing anymore: it's Russian roulette.

Chasing the hot manager, the hot sector or the hot industry is a very powerful mood-altering drug...until you overdose, and it kills you. Underdiversification is for hares. Disciplined diversification—hitting the ball long and straight down the middle of the fairway—is for tortoises. Guess who always wins?

☠ EUPHORIA

This is what I call it, anyway. Academics seem to like to label it "overconfidence," and many advisors—after a long, exhausting day of trying to calm its victims—just call it "greed." However one labels it, it's essentially the loss of an adult sense of principal risk.

Americans seem to think that, as the equity market rises (which, remember, it does nearly four years in five), the risk of a significant decline is diminishing. (And, as we'll see when we look at the very next Big Mistake, they think that risk is rising as markets fall precipitously). The opposite is true, of course, but that's not even my point.

The point is that, when people forget completely about principal risk, and just worry about being "outperformed" by someone else, you've entered the euphoria zone. Early in 2000, I actually met an advisor who was being sued by a client whose diversified portfolio had returned 29% in 1999. Seems the client played bridge with a couple of people who'd been up 80% that year—suicidally underdiversifying in NASDAQ, of course.

(Note that underdiversification and euphoria—and a couple of other Big Mistakes we've yet to get to—can be and usually are made simultaneously. Just because you've caught one fatal disease doesn't mean you're immune to all the others.)

☠ PANIC

Thoroughly explored in Chapter Three, so we don't have to belabor it here. The two critical things to remember are that (1) panic is a Big Mistake, but it's clearly not the only one, and (2) panic always rationalizes itself. "I have to get out until we see who wins the election/we see how the war in Afghanistan goes/we get past the housing depression/the unemployment rate comes down/we get the deficit under control/deflation/inflation/OPEC/Watergate/Vietnam/Ike's second heart attack/Pearl Harbor..."

There's always a reason—usually some current events "crisis" or other—and it's never really The Reason. It's a towel you wrap around yourself so the world won't see your naked fear. You can't deal effectively with panic until you acknowledge that you're panicking. And at that point—bless her—your advisor/coach will remind you that it's perfectly OK to feel the fear. But that it's never, never OK to act on the fear.

☠ SPECULATING WHEN YOU THINK YOU'RE STILL INVESTING, AND NOT REALIZING THAT YOU'VE CROSSED THE LINE

In 1999, normally rational people were walking around saying things like, "I'm investing in the future of e-commerce." Tripping out on euphoric underdiversification, they failed to notice that they weren't in Kansas anymore.

Here's what e-commerce "investors" were actually doing. (1) They were putting money into a business model which had not even existed three years earlier. (2) That business had yet to turn a profit; indeed, the industry leaders professed a strategy of deliberately losing increasing amounts of money to build market share—referred to, with marvelously unconscious humor, as "hits." (3) Moreover, folks were buying stock in recently started companies (or mutual funds thereof) which might or might not survive and thrive *even if the essential business model eventually worked.*

These were the very same people who ended up chasing real estate in 2005, oil when it spiked in 2008, and gold (not to mention bonds) in 2010.

There's a word for what they were doing. Hint: it isn't "investment." It's *speculation.* And what you have to remember to ask yourself—or at least allow your advisor/coach to ask you—the next time a "new era" rolls around is simply this. Never mind how intelligent the speculation seems at the moment: what percentage of your core capital (funds for retirement, education, legacies) should *ever* be invested in *any* speculation? My blissfully unscientific guess is that that simple question might have saved somewhere between two and three trillion of the seven trillion dollars that went up the flue when the dot.com music stopped in 2000.

"Investment" has to do with the identification of value. *Speculation is invariably a bet on the continuation of a price trend.* Price and value are always inversely correlated. Print this syllogism out in gothic lettering, and tape it up over the desk where you sit and ponder your portfolio.

If you're buying anything (much less anybody) because it beat everything else around for the last four or five years, (a) you're speculating on the continuation of a price trend, not investing in intrinsic value, and (b) you are about to get your head handed to you. All performance chasing is, by definition, speculation.

All short-term trading is also speculation, as are all derivatives: puts and calls, commodity futures, and the like. Anything whose price is directly tied to the price of something else, and which has no intrinsic value of its own, is a speculation. A Treasury bond is an investment, but an interest rate futures contract is a speculation. Wal-Mart common stock is an investment, but the Wal-Mart September 40 call option on the CBOE is a speculation. Even physical gold is an investment—a simply dreadful one, barring hyperinflation, but an investment nonetheless—while the December futures contract for the delivery of gold is a speculation (in that on the first trading day of January, it is guaranteed to be worthless).

☠ INVESTING FOR YIELD INSTEAD OF FOR TOTAL RETURN

Another golden oldie, fully sliced and diced in Chapter Four. One mo' time: do you want to try to take 5% a year for the next thirty years from an asset class whose total return has been 6%? Or might it be safer, *in the truest sense*, to try getting 5% from an asset class whose blended total return has been 10%–12%?

☠ LETTING YOUR COST BASIS DICTATE YOUR INVESTMENT DECISIONS

I've seen a fair number of people, over my four and a half decades in professional investing, who built—or just fell into—great fortunes in one spectacularly successful stock, which ultimately got to be 80%, 90% and more of their portfolio. Then they gave it all back by refusing to pay capital gains taxes (which are usually a fraction of income taxes) in order to return to proper diversification.

By the same token, I've seen—and continue to see—people who won't let go of obvious portfolio mistakes because "I can't take the loss," or "I have to wait to get even." Heaven knows how great the returns of quality investments will be while these people are waiting to get bailed out of their garbage.

Your investments don't know what you paid for them, and wouldn't act any differently if they did. Forget your cost; it's yesterday's news. Just keep migrating toward quality and diversification, and all good things will come to you in the fullness of time.

☠ LEVERAGE

There's a very good intellectual/economic case to be made for leverage, and it runs along these lines: if you can borrow against your house at, say, 6%, write off the interest on your tax return, and invest the borrowings in an asset class whose total long-term return is in the range of 10%–12%, you're smart to do so.

And on some planet in some galaxy somewhere, whose inhabitants invest rationally all the time, this argument is a certified humdinger.

Here on Planet Earth, it doesn't seem to work so well. People take second mortgages at, say, 6%, to buy Amazon.com at 209 in 1999, just about the time it starts tail-spinning toward 18. Or oil at $140 in 2008, just before it goes back to $30. Right again, dear reader: leverage is a song that mostly gets sung in toxic four-part harmony with underdiversification, euphoria and (unconscious) speculation.

Granted, leverage is a particularly seductive form of the Big Mistake. Because whereas the other manifestations can never work, leverage—done right—should. But this is a discussion of how things are in the real world, rather than how they should be. And done wrong—as it almost always is—leverage just ends up magnifying a number of other Big Mistakes.

❧

Thus concludes not just this chapter, but virtually the entire book. I'll have a few valedictory words of attitudinal guidance for you in just a moment, but you now know everything of paramount importance that I know, and everything I set out to tell you.

I promised you at the beginning of the book that most of what you wanted to learn about mutual funds—which comes down to superior selection and/or timing—was essentially unknowable, and didn't matter anyway. I further promised you not that your mutual funds would "outperform" your neighbors' mutual funds, but that you would achieve a financial outcome superior to that of your neighbors. I consider my obligation to you, pursuant to those two promises, fully discharged at this point. (If you don't agree, I'll bet it's because you did exactly what I asked you not to do in the Preface: you started fighting the book before you'd read it all the way through just once. So now, either you go back and read it through again, or we have to agree to disagree, and part friends.)

Finally, I promised that you would ultimately see the true value in an advisor/coach's counsel for what it really is: the presence in your life of someone who will consistently talk you out of making The Big Mistake.

There's not much left for me to do, then, but to wish you the friendship and guidance of that caring advisor, and the joys of faith, patience and discipline.

Just Remember

- In real life, mutual fund "performance" statistics are an abstraction, because people don't get investment returns. They get investor returns, which are much, much worse.

- Unaided by behavioral coaching, the investor sooner or later (or both) gets done in by the hard-wired emotional propensity to make The Big Mistake. As Pogo Possum wisely observed, all those years ago, "We have met the enemy, and he is us."

- Most of what you need to know about building and maintaining an intelligent mutual fund portfolio can be summed up in five words: get diversified and stay diversified. Diversification immunizes you against The Big Mistake more effectively than does any other single discipline.

- A nicely diversified equity fund portfolio might look something like this:

Large-cap growth	Small-cap growth
Large-cap value	Small-cap value

International/emerging markets

- When you're dollar-cost averaging evenly into that kind of portfolio, you're always loading up on whatever's out of favor, and just pecking at stuff that's become fashionably expensive. This is exactly the opposite of what most people do, which largely explains why most people don't achieve wealth.

- (A) The less often you change your mutual fund portfolio, the better return you'll get in the long run. (B) Trying to increase your real-life return a lot by switching funds is like trying to improve your personality by changing your socks. (C) Immediate past performance (say, five years or less) is the single worst way to select mutual funds ever hallucinated by the mind of man. (D) Portfolio management is the tail. Behavior is the dog. (E) Everything else is a refinement.

- The Big Mistake has eight incarnations. Many of the Eight Great Mistakes can be made simultaneously, and a couple are usually made sequentially.

- The Eight Great Mistakes are:

- *Overdiversification:* owning nothing by owning everything.

- *Underdiversification:* the fatal narrowing of a portfolio down to essentially one idea.

- *Euphoria:* the loss of an adult sense of principal risk.
- *Panic:* the failure of faith in the face of the apocalypse *du jour.*
- *Speculating when you still think you're investing:* the siren song of a "new era," and of chasing hot price trends instead of intrinsic value.
- *Investing for yield instead of for total return:* suicide on the installment plan, by fixing one's income in contemplation of thirty years of rising living costs.
- *Letting your cost basis dictate your investment decisions:* asking your investments to behave differently because of what you paid for them.
- *Leverage:* hocking the house to buy the wrong idea at the wrong time.
- *Just once more: if all your advisor ever did was to stop you from tap-dancing into that minefield—over and over again—how many multiples of what you pay her is she really worth?*

Epilogue

OPTIMISM IS THE ONLY REALISM

At the bottom of the postcard pictured on page 153, I snuck in a postscript: an idea which, though not previously addressed in any detail, is critical to the program outlined in this book.

No one can plan for the future—much less invest successfully in it—without believing in that future. And this becomes my working definition of optimism: an abiding faith in the future.

And I'm not speaking here of starry-eyed optimism or blind faith. I don't advocate hope for the future in spite of present reality, but because of it. Indeed, I maintain that optimism is the only realism, in that it is the only worldview which squares with the facts, and with the historical record.

Pessimism, on the other hand, is deeply counterintuitive, because no one examining history would arrive at a declinist worldview. Thus, for me, pessimism is a lot like race hatred: no one would ever generate it spontaneously. Someone has to teach it to you.

The man who writes to you is barely in his sixty-eighth year, but the geopolitical, technological and economic progress that's taken place in my lifetime probably exceeds, in quality and quantity, all previous human advances.

In 1918, along with half a million other Americans and some

20 million people worldwide, my father's older sister died of influenza. Today we joke about whether or not to get a flu shot this year—and if we *do* get the flu, we merely fret about missing a few day's work.

There are a dozen diseases—tuberculosis and polio, to name two—which were common killers and cripplers at the beginning of my life, and which have been all but eradicated. You cannot be my age and not have been ill six times in your life with maladies that would have killed you had you been born even 50 years earlier. No wonder U.S. life expectancy went from 47 in 1900 to 66 in 1950 to 78 in the year 2000.

Geopolitically, the world always looks as if it has insuperable problems—fundamentalist terrorism, genocide in Africa—but the fact is that today's world is almost immeasurably safer than the one I came into, and in which I grew up.

I was born about two-thirds of the way through humankind's most terrible war. It was, in every sense, a world war, which began on September 1, 1939, when Hitler invaded Poland, and ended six years and one day later, on September 2, 1945, when the Japanese signed the instrument of surrender. *And on every single day of those six years, that war killed an average of over 26,000 people.*

Then one day in October 1962, when I was just 19, I sat in

a classroom at Columbia University. My economics professor was lecturing—it was probably a pretty good lecture, too—but I wasn't listening. I was looking out the window at a heartbreakingly beautiful New York autumn day, and waiting to see if I was going to die. I didn't take it personally, because I knew that, if I died, so would just about everyone else on the planet. For this was the Cuban Missile Crisis, and for a few days there was a pretty good chance that the species was going to extinguish itself in a total thermonuclear war.

The world didn't end that day, but the Cold War balance of terror defined global geopolitics for another quarter of a century—until, on November 9, 1989, the modern world was born. On that day, the Berlin Wall came down, amid the death throes of communism. Liberty won, not least of all because liberty can't lose.

No one will choose oppression instead of liberty, or poverty instead of plenty, once he's *seen* liberty and plenty, and once he's realized that he and his fellow citizens have—or ought to have—a choice.

Soviet totalitarianism could only survive as long as it was able to convince the inmates of its dungeon that capitalism left people worse off. So if it didn't let people travel to the West, and if it kept jamming television signals from the free world, it could maintain the fiction.

Once those television signals started bouncing off satellites, and the inmates couldn't be prevented from seeing them any longer, the game was over. When everyone could see that democratic, free-market capitalism produces an immeasurably higher standard of living, the emperor could be seen to be wearing no clothes. (Boris Yeltsin, the first post-Soviet Russian leader, was said to have had his epiphany in the middle of a huge supermarket in Texas.) In the long run, something like this process—powerfully magnified by the Internet—has to happen throughout much of the Middle East, and in Africa.

And speaking of the Internet, let's not forget that, if the defining geopolitical event of our time happened little more than 20 years ago, the greatest technological invention of *all* time happened well within the lives of the majority of people reading this book.

It was, of course, the microprocessor—the entire computer on a tiny chip. The microprocessor was invented in 1971, and has doubled in computing power (or halved in cost, whichever way you care to look at it) about every two years since. From ATMs to anti-lock brakes to the personal computer to the Hubble Space Telescope to (most particularly) the Internet, the microprocessor defines modernity.

Indeed, it is already possible to see a huge gulf between all of human technological progress to 1971, and all that's happened since. If you doubt this, or if you just can't conceive of it in concrete terms, treat yourself to the movie *Apollo 13.* And watch as the smartest rocket scientists in the world try to figure out how to get those three astronauts safely home using *slide rules*. Because this was April 1970, and the microprocessor was still a year away.

The computer in the BlackBerry or iPhone you carry today is a million times smaller, a million times cheaper, and a thousand times more powerful than all the computing power that was available to NASA the night the Apollo 13 exploded. Over the next quarter century or so, that billionfold increase in computing power per dollar will happen again. As it does, information technology may very well solve all our current problems, including (but certainly not limited to) poverty, disease, energy and the environment.

The Internet's great contribution to the furtherance of liberty is that it purely democratizes all the information. All oppressive regimes lie to their people in order to cover up their ineptitude, corruption, and criminality. But if you can get on the Internet—as virtually everyone in the world will be able to do over the next several years—you can find out the truth. And not just by reading about it, but by actually seeing and listening to it. "And you shall know the truth, and the truth shall make you free." This is the great thing—maybe the greatest thing—we democratic capitalist truth-tellers have going for us. And it's exactly what will ultimately bring down today's lying hate-mongers, just as it brought down communism.

This is the truth. And the one thing of which we can be absolutely sure regarding the truth is that you will never see it on the news. For even as the *outlets* of news have proliferated wildly (on cable and the web), news *coverage* seems to me to have shrunk down to one story at a time. And that story is always, always bad.

There is virtually always an apocalypse *du jour* going on somewhere in our world. And on the rare occasions when there is not, journalism will simply invent one, and present it 24/7 as the incipient end of the world.

Thus, the news is always and everywhere antithetical to the truth. And if history must make optimists of us all, there are days on which the news can make a pessimist out of just about anyone.

So, you must choose: the truth shall make you free. Or the news will drive you crazy. The fuel on which all successful wealth-building in equities runs is optimism.

And optimism is the only realism.

BIBLIOGRAPHY

The ideal companion volume to this book—particularly for those still struggling with my contention that equities are the "safest" long-term investment—is Jeremy Siegel's *Stocks for the Long Run.*

Two very good books for the general reader on economic reality versus rampant pessimism are Brian Wesbury's *It's Not As Bad As You Think* and Steve Forbes's *How Capitalism Will Save Us.*

Successful equity investing, as we've seen so often in this book, depends on one's ability to resist the market's excesses of euphoria followed by panic. Try to read some of the literature of both, for perspective.

Probably the best book we will ever have by a victim of a "new era" bubble is David Denby's memoir of the dot.com madness, *American Sucker.* Denby's dispassionate, deeply honest account of how he got caught up in the tech mania is a cautionary classic. Two other important histories of the great bull market of the 1990s and its terrible aftermath are John Cassidy's *Dot.con*, which focuses specifically on the Internet, and Roger Lowenstein's *Origins of the Crash.*

And a couple of good reads on the subprime mortgage cataclysm and its global financial and economic effects in 2007–2009 are Lowenstein's rather hyperbolically titled *The End of Wall Street* and David Wessel's *In Fed We Trust.*

Charles Kindleberger's *Manias, Panics and Crashes* is the best formal examination of the cycle of bubbles and crashes through the ages. It is a fairly demanding exercise, however, and you may decide you'd prefer a more colorful, less rigorous tour of the Tulip Mania, the South Sea Bubble, and the Roaring Twenties, among other episodes. In that case, you can look at Edward Chancellor's *Devil Take the Hindmost.*

Finally, read David McCullough's biography of Harry Truman. It doesn't bear directly on markets or investments; it's just good for your soul.

GLOSSARY

active management – the practice of attempting to cause one's portfolio to return more than the benchmark index of that portfolio, either through superior stock selection or by becoming more or less fully invested.

asset allocation – the spreading of risk and reward which attends upon the purchase of securities in different asset classes—stocks, bonds and cash equivalents—as opposed to *diversification*.

asset class – the totality of a given type of security, e.g. common stocks, bonds, and/or cash equivalents.

basis point – one one-hundredth of one percent. If the bellwether 10-year Treasury bond goes from a 3.05% yield to 3.10%, its yield is said to have risen five basis points.

bear market – a major decline in stock and/or bond prices, usually defined as a decline of at least 20% in the relevant market index from a previous high.

bond – a borrowing, secured to the lender by the borrower's promise to pay interest and/or principal at certain dates. In corporate finance, the debt of a corporation. Used interchangeably in this book with the phrase *fixed-income investment* and the word *debt*.

bull market – a major rise in stock and/or bond prices, sometimes defined as an increase of at least 20% in the relevant market index from a previous bear market low; also, a market that is trading in new high ground.

capital – the amount of one's principal as opposed to the income expected from that principal.

capitalization-weighted (or ***cap-weighted***) – describes a stock index weighted for the total stock value of each company in the index. It therefore skews the index to be hugely affected by the price action of the very largest companies in the index. If you had a cap-weighted index of six companies, one of whose stocks was worth a total of $10 billion and the other five worth $2 billion each, half of each day's change in the index would be caused by the one largest company.

capitalize – in financial/investment planning, one divides a needed level of income by the percentage one believes one's portfolio can reasonably return, in order to arrive at the capital value required to produce the needed income. An income of $50,000, capitalized at (i.e. divided by) 5%, equals $1,000,000 of capital necessary.

cash – as a portfolio holding, usually a cash equivalent: a security which is highly liquid, has a known market value and has a maturity date, when acquired, less than three months away.

Also, a pool of such securities, e.g. a money market fund.

CD – a bank certificate of deposit, or debt instrument issued to a depositor for a specific length of time and usually with a fixed rate of interest. Like other deposits in participating banks, CDs are guaranteed (within limits) by the Federal Deposit Insurance Corporation (FDIC), a federal agency established in 1933.

Chicago Board Options Exchange (CBOE) – the world's largest options exchange, trading standardized option contracts on stocks, indexes, interest rates and ETFs.

closed-end funds – equity portfolios having a fixed number of publicly traded shares. Purchases are made from, and sales made to, other investors rather than to and from the issuer as in open-end mutual funds. The price of shares in the open market may represent a premium or a discount to the fund's net asset value, whereas all transactions in open-end mutual funds are based on net asset value.

common stock – ownership of a corporation, represented by shares that are a claim on the corporation's earnings and assets; usually entitles the holder to vote on the affairs of the corporation. Used interchangeably in this book with the words *stocks* and *equities.*

compounding – earnings realized on both principal and

earnings that were realized earlier. As the pool of capital expands, the same percentage return adds commensurately more wealth to that pool.

conservative – adjective used in this book to describe an asset class which has demonstrated superior long-term effectiveness at conserving *purchasing power*, i.e. real wealth. By this definition, stocks are more conservative than bonds.

correction – a moderate decline in stock and/or bond prices, usually defined as a decline of at least 10% but less than 20% in the relevant market index from a previous high.

CPI – the Consumer Price Index, a measure of the change in prices of a fixed basket of goods bought by a typical consumer, including food, shelter, utilities, transportation, medical care and other items. The CPI is computed, and published monthly, by the Bureau of Labor Statistics of the U.S. Department of Labor.

debt – see *bond*

derivative – a financial instrument—usually an agreement between two parties—whose value is determined by the price of something else, such as a stock, an index, a commodity or a currency.

diversification – the spreading of risk and reward which attends upon the purchase of different types of securities within the same asset class, as opposed to *asset allocation*. Examples: purchasing bonds (or bond funds) of different quality issuers and/or different maturity dates; purchasing U.S. and foreign and/or large- and small-company stocks or stock funds.

dividend – generally, the distribution of part of a corporation's earnings to its shareholders.

dollar-cost averaging – a method of accumulating assets by investing the same dollar amount in the same securities at regular intervals. The investor thus buys more shares at relatively low prices and fewer shares at relatively high prices. This results in a lower average cost than if the investor regularly bought the same number of shares.

Dow Jones Industrial Average – a price-weighted average of thirty very large publicly traded stocks; the oldest and most widely quoted of all market indicators. The thirty stocks in the DJIA usually represent 15% to 20% of the market value of all New York Stock Exchange-listed stocks.

EAFE – MSCI Barra's Europe, Australasia, Far East Equity index, a benchmark for managers of international stock portfolios.

equities – see *common stocks*

equity premium – a concept of the incremental return of stocks over bonds (because of concomitant equity volatility) which persists over long periods of time.

Exchange Traded Funds (ETFs) – investment funds which trade on a stock exchange and which hold assets such as stocks, commodities and bonds. ETFs normally trade at about the net asset value of their underlying assets over the course of the trading day.

expense ratio – the total dollar expenses incurred by a mutual fund or other managed/pooled investment divided by its total assets. In general, investments with lower *portfolio turnover* will achieve a lower expense ratio, though turnover is by no means a fund's only major expense.

fixed income investment – see *bond*

growth stock – a stock which is valued for its ability to grow its earnings rapidly and consistently, rather than for the relationship of its assets to its stock price. Growth stocks usually sell for higher price-earnings multiples than do more cyclical *value stocks.* A growth stock is a growth stock until the company's growth stalls—at which point it may (or may not) become a value stock. Ford was a growth stock until the car market got saturated; then it became a value stock. IBM was once the ultimate growth stock, lost its way and became a value stock—and is now a growth stock once again. Remember: this is finance, not physics.

interest – the cost of borrowed money, paid by a borrower to a lender.

liquid – securities and/or markets in which large purchases and sales can be made quickly and easily with negligible effect on the price of the securities/markets. Thus, the U.S. stock market is far more liquid than that of Malaysia or Singapore, and the stock of a very large company is much more liquid than that of a very small one.

market timing – the purchase and/or sale of securities based primarily if not solely on the expectation of a general rise or fall in a market (or in a market sector), as opposed to investment based on the intrinsic fundamental value of securities (or one's perception thereof). Market timing is thus a form of *speculation* rather than of investment.

money – in the short run, the sum of one's cash, cash equivalents, and readily marketable investments. In the long run, *purchasing power.*

mutual fund – an open-end investment company which pools investor funds and manages the investment of those funds, usually to a specific purpose or end. A mutual fund has a floating number of outstanding shares because it stands ready to sell or redeem shares at their current *net asset value.*

NASDAQ Composite Index – a stock market index of the common stocks and similar securities listed on the NASDAQ stock market. The index has over 3,000 components, and is closely followed as an indicator of the performance of technology and other growth issues.

net asset value (NAV) – the current market value of the shares of a *mutual fund*, at which price the fund stands ready to redeem (and, in the case of a fund with no sales charge, to sell) its shares. NAV is calculated daily by most funds; the closing market prices of all the fund's securities holdings are added to all other assets (typically cash), all liabilities are subtracted, and the result (total net assets) is divided by the total number of fund shares outstanding.

Nifty Fifty – colloquially, the fifty or so very largest, most visible growth stocks. In times of great enthusiasm (e.g. 1995-99) and great revulsion (e.g. 1973–74) the Nifty Fifty have often outrun the overall market—in both directions.

nominal return – the stated or implied percentage return of an asset in constant dollars, unadjusted for inflation. A $1000 bond which pays $80 in annual interest provides an 8% nominal return; a stock that rises in price from $100 to $110 in a year has provided a 10% nominal return. See *real return.*

passive investing – creation and maintenance of a portfolio which, as nearly as possible, replicates its benchmark index.

portfolio turnover – the extent to which a fund manager sells securities out of his portfolio in order to buy other securities. Generally, the higher the level of turnover, the higher a fund's *expense ratio.*

principal – in practical terms, the sum of the market values of all one's investments; also, the face value of one's debt investments, as distinguished from the interest payable thereon.

purchasing power – the value of money as measured by the goods and services it can buy. This book uses purchasing power as the long-term definition of *money.*

real return – the nominal (stated or implied) percentage return of an asset less inflation. A bond that pays 6% interest when inflation is 3% has a 3% real return. See *nominal return.*

risk – in general, the chance of a long-term, irreversible diminution in one's wealth; also, the chance that one will be forced to dispose of an investment at a temporarily depressed price. In this book, which defines wealth as long-term *purchasing power, bonds* are held to be high-risk investments, because they have historically been at best marginally effective in preserving purchasing power.

Russell 2000 – a market capitalization-weighted index of small-capitalization stocks, computed and published by Frank Russell Company of Tacoma, WA. The 1000 largest publicly traded companies are in the Russell 1000 Index, which acts a lot like the S&P 500; the Russell 2000 is made up of the next 2000 companies.

safety – generally, the probability of maintaining the value of one's wealth. Since this book defines wealth as long-term *purchasing power*, stocks are held to afford a relatively high level of long-term safety, in that they have historically enhanced purchasing power.

S&P 500 – The Standard & Poor's Composite Index of 500 Stocks. A market value-weighted index measuring the change in the total market value of 500 of the largest publicly traded stocks relative to the base period 1941–43. The S&P 500 accounts for roughly three quarters of all the publicly traded equity in the U.S.

separately managed account – an individual investment account as distinct from a commingled account like a mutual fund, with a customized portfolio formulated for a particular investor's specific investment objectives and/or desired restrictions, and professionally managed. SMAs are usually offered with a minimum investment of $100,000.

speculation – the purchase and/or sale of securities based primarily if not solely on the expectation of a change in market price as opposed to a change in intrinsic value.

stocks – see *common stocks*

systematic withdrawal – the practice of taking fixed withdrawals from a pool of capital at regular intervals. As long as the amount/percentage being withdrawn is sufficiently less than the total earnings of the pool of capital, both the amounts withdrawn and the capital itself can continue to grow.

total return – the sum of the cash distribution of a security and the price appreciation (or depreciation) of that security. A stock which rises in price from $50 to $55 per share in a year while paying a dividend of $1 per share has provided a total return in that year of 12%.

value stock – typically, a company in a relatively mature and/or commodity industry, whose earnings cycle with the economy, and/or with the waxing and waning of that industry. Paper, chemical, oil and automobile stocks are classic value stocks, and investors try to anticipate where they are in their cycles. When the market gets so excited that it starts pricing a value industry as if it were a *growth* industry (e.g. oil in 1979-81, just before OPEC collapsed, and in early 2008), it is usually a sign that the gargoyles have taken over the cathedral.

variable annuity – a contract with a life insurance company in which the company agrees to make periodic payments to the contract holder immediately or at some future date. The buildup of cash value inside a variable annuity is tax-deferred, and all the earnings are taxed at ordinary income tax rates when and as they are withdrawn. Most variable annuities are available with a death benefit which assures the return of original principal even if the then-current market value of the contract is less, and/or with a guaranteed minimum stream of future income potentially beyond that which the contract value will support; both these insurances come at an additional premium cost.

variable universal life insurance – a form of permanent life insurance in which the cash values can be invested in a wide variety of investment accounts similar to mutual funds.

Wilshire 5000 Total Market Index – the broadest index for the U.S. equity market, the Wilshire 5000 purports to measure the performance of all U.S. equity securities with readily available price data.

yield – the stated cash distribution of a security divided by its price. Not to be confused with total return. Generally, the higher a security's current yield, the lower its total return; e.g. bonds yield more than stocks, and have a much lower total return.

ACKNOWLEDGMENTS

My life is my family and my work. It has been inexpressibly enriched by the fact that the best person I have ever known—the former Joan Carrick—married me. Our firstborn daughter Karen, a sought-after financial writer and editor in her own right, has always been my most astute editor—and critic. Our daughter Joan Eileen, to whom this edition is dedicated, keeps my company's accounts while pursuing her own dreams. Our son Mark manages the distribution of my books, and always has my back. Karen's and her husband David Dickerson's two children, Rebecca and Will Dickerson, taught me that I was born to be 'Pa; the lesson is ongoing. My bride and I are Rebecca's and Will's riverkeepers, employing every principle and practice in the book you've just read, to blessed effect.

ABOUT THE AUTHOR

©MARK PATRICK MURRAY

Nick Murray was born in the borough of Queens in the City of New York in 1943, and began his career in the financial advisory profession in 1967. He has written eleven books for financial services professionals since 1987. *Simple Wealth, Inevitable Wealth* is his only book for the individual investor.

Nick was the 2007 recipient of the Malcolm S. Forbes Public Awareness Award for Excellence in Advancing Financial Understanding.